CHRONICLES *of* HISTORIC BROOKLYN

CHRONICLES *of*
HISTORIC
BROOKLYN

JOHN B. MANBECK

Charleston   London

THE
History
PRESS

Published by The History Press
Charleston, SC 29403
www.historypress.net

Copyright © 2013 by John B. Manbeck
All rights reserved

Cover images courtesy of John Manbeck.

First published 2013

Manufactured in the United States

ISBN 978.1.60949.959.4

Library of Congress CIP data applied for.

CONTENTS

FOREWORD

Nearly every page of Brooklyn's storied history is filled with incredible characters—from longshoremen to labor leaders, storekeepers to soldiers, writers, waiters, strivers and schemers. In other words, real Brooklynites doing their best to fulfill the American Dream. From its beginning as the seventeenth-century Dutch settlement Breuckelen to its rise as America's third-largest city in the nineteenth century and its prominence today as—among other things—one of the hippest places on the planet, Brooklyn has long been the place for dreamers, inventors and creators. It's a place where prosperity comes to those willing to think big and work hard. When it comes to chronicling the character and characters of this great borough, who better than historian, author, educator and Brooklynite John Manbeck to take on the task? In addition to his distinguished career as a professor of English at Brooklyn's own Kingsborough Community College, John was the official Brooklyn Borough historian from 1993 to 2002—and that means John knows Brooklyn through and through.

In his weekly column "Historically Speaking" in the *Brooklyn Eagle*, John took readers on the fantastic journey that is Brooklyn. Since I believe that Brooklyn is the closest thing here on earth to the Promised Land, it's exciting to be able to revisit John's writing in this single volume.

John remembers some of Brooklyn's most important and beloved activists, like Evelyn and Everett Ortner, who spearheaded the renovation of Brooklyn brownstones in the early 1960s, and Joan Maynard, who led the preservation efforts of the Weeksville Heritage Center, a nineteenth-

Brooklyn Borough President Marty Markowitz on the Brooklyn Bridge. *Photo by Kathryn Kirk.*

century settlement of free blacks. (Brooklyn, of course, actively participated in the abolitionist movement, with sites in downtown Brooklyn playing a role in the Underground Railroad). The wonderful Olga Bloom is also remembered. She was the pioneer of one of Brooklyn's—and all of New York City's—most unique music venues, having created a floating concert hall at the Fulton Ferry Landing called Bargemusic way back in 1976.

Along with prominent Brooklynites, John's columns remind us of what a truly special place Brooklyn was and continues to be. It's a place that, even though called the "Borough of Churches," still has room for religions of every kind. It's a place where the great-grandkids of the children who once cheered on Brooklyn Dodger Jackie Robinson at Ebbets Field now cheer on Brooklyn Net Deron Williams at Barclays Center. John takes readers to some of Brooklyn's fabulous green spaces, from the historic Brooklyn Botanic Garden to newcomer Brooklyn Bridge Park, and from Fort Greene Park to the Brooklyn Promenade. And hold onto your hats as you journey back in time to go ice skating in the park or swimming in the pool at the Hotel St. George—America's largest saltwater pool in the 1940s and '50s.

Brooklyn was also home to America's largest restaurant, Lundy's, which in its heyday could seat more than two thousand patrons. Take a ride on the antique steeds of the magnificent Jane's Carousel, now housed in a spectacular pavilion in DUMBO designed by Pritzker Prize–winning French architect Jean Nouvel. No matter where John takes readers, whether it be Brooklyn during the Civil War or a twenty-first-century urban farm, he does so with insight, intelligence and sheer love of the borough he knows so well.

John Manbeck has written a true love letter to Brooklyn, and whether you're in Brooklyn by birthright or because you were smart enough to make the move here, you're bound to enjoy this ode to the greatest borough. (Let's face it, where else but Brooklyn and Junior's can you get the quintessentially American cheesecake experience?) And for you Brooklyn "wannabes" and "couldabeens" (after all, one out of seven Americans can trace their roots to Brooklyn), after dipping into some of these marvelous reminiscences, you're likely to want to become an actual Brooklynite, too. Because, truth be told, Brooklyn is really the heartland of America!

—*Brooklyn Borough President Marty Markowitz*

INTRODUCTION

Brooklyn is all grown up now. Since the opening of the twenty-first century, Brooklyn has renewed its population with an influx of multiethnic young people endowed with a fresh, creative outlook. Newly constructed skyscrapers downtown reflect a mirror challenge to the City Across the River. A bold, rasping sports arena reintroduced a competitive entertainment venue that has worried Manhattan. The fall Brooklyn Book Festival captured the former "New York Is Book Country" and added more verve, time and focus. The Brooklyn Academy of Music (BAM), the Brooklyn Museum, the Brooklyn Historical Society, the Brooklyn public libraries and other quasi-official institutions enliven a cultural scene that was envisioned at the close of the nineteenth century, back when Brooklyn was a standalone city.

But as history tells us, the City of Brooklyn already had created "excellent hospitals and schools, literary institutions and libraries," according to the venerable *Brooklyn Eagle*. Using that institution as a soapbox, I produced a weekly column titled "Historically Speaking" for fifty weeks a year for eight years. This was my retirement project after I departed from Kingsborough Community College, where I taught English and journalism for thirty-two years, as well as a follow-up to my eight years as Brooklyn Borough Historian. My appreciation goes to the *Eagle*'s current publisher, John Dozier Hasty, who encouraged me to write and add feature stories to my dossier. My two guiding themes decreed that I include "Brooklyn" and "history" as a motif for each column. Sometimes I stretched this goal if I wished to make a point, but I had fun relating contemporary news to Brooklyn's glamorous history.

John Manbeck. *Guisinger Photography.*

I used the institutions of government—police, fire, politics—to show how Brooklyn worked and how it changed. As a middle-class suburb, a popular niche in sports, industry and entertainment was created, producing a unique reputation. That permanent hallmark eventually sold the borough as a commodity in that the name "Brooklyn" has assumed a life of its own.

In the first series of columns I collected for *Brooklyn: Historically Speaking* (The History Press, 2008), I excerpted topics that I felt explained the origins of New York's most populous suburb and the challenges it faced. In the last four years, time has pushed Brooklyn significantly higher in recognition. I knew I had merely skimmed the historic surface. With this volume, I have tried to fill in the blanks: its great parks, its devotion to sports and food, the quirks of holiday celebrations, the astounding growth patterns of gentrification, the underbelly of criminal activity in the borough, its heroic stand during World War II, a second look at Coney Island and a fond farewell to several of Brooklyn's more influential voices. With changes forced on us by nature as well as by developers, it is prudent to remember and preserve as much of the past as is feasible. This legacy we bestow on newcomers who follow.

These columns appear mostly as they were printed in the *Eagle*, with minor editorial adjustments and corrections. They have been reorganized and grouped in thematic clusters. The original publication dates appear under the titles.

No creative production stands alone; support creates belief in the project. Marty Markowitz, the ebullient Brooklyn Borough president, has been the public voice of the borough for the past three terms of office. I knew him from his days as state senator when he gave me a citation for my extracurricular work in founding the Kingsborough Historical Society. He is a vociferous voice of Brooklyn and will be sorely missed after his term. Marty has graciously written the foreword to this book.

I asked a co-worker from the *Brooklyn Eagle*, Henrik Krogius, editor of *The Heights Press*, to write the afterword. I admire Henrik for many reasons: his journalistic skills, his successful career as a newspaperman and photographer, his devout historical interest in Brooklyn Heights, his gentlemanly manners. Henrik has published a magnificent coffee-table book of New York photographs he took over a fifty-year period titled *New York: You're a Wonderful Town*, as well as a volume for The History Press on the origins of the Brooklyn Promenade. We have one more alliance. In the 1960s, I taught at Helsinki University on a Fulbright grant. While working at the *Eagle*, I discovered that Henrik was born in Finland, another feather in his cap.

Other names behind the publication of this book include the librarians and researchers who aided with information and pictures, namely Joy Holland and Ivy Marvel of Brooklyn Public Library's Brooklyn Collection and the anonymous researchers at the Library of Congress and the Smithsonian Institution. Adam Klein filled the role of my most capable indexer. Production Manager at the *Eagle*, Artur Ramus, added polish to the original articles and graphics.

My interest in Brooklyn's history started with the Kingsborough Historical Society, guided by former students Gail Smollon, John Rossi and Lorraine Tondi Insana. The editors at The History Press, particularly Whitney Tarella Landis and Will Collicott, guided me through the technical forest. My son, Brooks, a photographer, gave me insight into the mysteries of DPI and TIFF.

But foremost, I thank my wife, Virginia, who is my prime proofreader and to whose support I owe whatever success I have achieved.

Part I

HISTORY

History Has Many Layers
April 15, 2002

Every person has a history. Our life stories become history. History is memory and is captured in genealogy, the history of our families. This study of our ancestors has grown increasingly popular in recent years. Libraries, archives, historical societies, genealogical organizations and historians process more and more requests in a search for our identities.

History is not buried in the past. The Delaware Indians left us with their names. Gowanus was a variation of an Indian chief's name. Canarsie was a sub-division of the Delaware nation. The Dutch traders who settled in Brooklyn gave us the name of the borough and its neighborhoods: Flatbush, New Utrecht, Greenpoint and Bushwick. They further enriched our language with words such as "stoop" and "boss." The English, who defeated the Dutch, brought in "Gravesend," "Kings County" and "New York." Each new ethnic group introduced new words and customs that enriched our language and culture.

We have adopted and adapted without realizing it. A neighborhood that was once German became Jewish, then Irish, then Italian and then Chinese. It's also known as the Lower East Side or the East Village. Each of these peoples brought its own history. I call it a "layered history."

In the nineteenth century and even more recently, many reactionaries were so afraid of change—of history—that they wanted to stop it. These people

Brooklyn Borough Hall, 1942. Photo by Edward Rutter. *Brooklyn Public Library, Brooklyn Collection.*

called themselves Nativists. They felt that America was for Americans and that they were the only pure Americans. They identified with the "Know Nothing" political party; they didn't want to know their own history. Their story has been told in Herbert Asbury's informal history *The Gangs of New York*, in which "American" gangs fought the immigrant Irish gangs.

Scare tactics still abound. Race and hate crimes reflect this mentality just as the draft riots of the Civil War did when blacks were lynched in New York and Brooklyn because they were seen as a threat to the white economy.

A study of layered history shows that diversity allows us to profit from history. The largest West Indian parade in the world takes place in Brooklyn each Labor Day weekend. It is our Mardi Gras, a wealth of joy and entertainment that would be lost if modern immigration were halted. In Williamsburg, the festival of the *giglio* allows us to observe an Italian Roman Catholic procession. The many Jewish holidays, both religious and festive, bring us new historic insights.

In addition to celebrations, foods and dress also enlighten us. When I was a child, pizza was foreign in my Brooklyn neighborhood. Now, pizza is delivered in boxes emblazoned with American flags. Mexican foods? Maybe in Texas or California, but certainly not in Brooklyn. All Chinese food was generically categorized as "chop suey." Certainly, no one knew what Arabs ate. No one would have thought of eating at a Thai, Indian or Indochinese (Vietnamese) restaurant.

Even today, while our tolerance has expanded, too often our thoughts of history are limited to images of men with white wigs and white faces. The Brooklyn Historical Society, Brooklyn Public Library, Brooklyn Museum, local historical societies and the borough president's office have taken steps, but we remain too provincial in Brooklyn. A more concerted effort must be made to include the history of all Brooklynites in our official layered history.

A Swell Party for the Brooklyn Bridge
May 29, 2008

"One hundred and twenty-five years old?"
"Why, it seemed like just yesterday she was born!"
"Doesn't look her age."
"My, my, how time flies!"

Star of stage, screen and legend, the Brooklyn Bridge—née the Great East River Bridge—posed for her birthday party the weekend of May 24 (with a preview blowout May 23 featuring candles, fire pyrotechnics, orchestral fanfare and all.)

A few of her starring roles in over twenty-two films include *It Happened in Brooklyn* (remember the love song "The Brooklyn Bridge"?) and the more recent *Enchanted*, although hosts of others from *A View from the Bridge* to Bugs Bunny can be found in her portfolio, including a script by F. Scott Fitzgerald written for Columbia Pictures in 1940 but never filmed. And you can add to those movies eight plays, several television tributes, over fifteen songs and more than twelve books, not to mention countless photographs and other visual arts.

And still she stands there ready for her profile, unbending as steel, solid as a rock. Loved but from a distance (at 113 Columbia Heights) by Colonel Washington Roebling, only thirty-two years old when he succeeded his father as builder. Remember her welcoming celebration? Wasn't she a beauty? Hasn't lost a bit of her charm. That was back in '83—1883, that is.

The Brooklyn Bridge song sheet autographed by the composers. *Photo by John Manbeck.*

Honored by the president of the United States (Chester Arthur), three governors (New Jersey, Rhode Island and New York—future president Grover Cleveland) and two mayors. Speeches, speeches, speeches to fifty thousand spectators. Three hours of speeches on peace, courage, science and commerce. But not by the president.

And then the fireworks—one hour of pyrotechnics from the bridge's towers and her center span. Fourteen tons of fireworks with over ten thousand pieces and five hundred rockets, all supplemented by a full moon. Fireworks supplied by Detwiller & Street Co.; the moon sponsored by the heavens. For subsequent lighting, pedestrians would be satisfied with the electric lights.

In Brooklyn, Mayor Seth Low (who had attempted to have Washington Roebling fired from the job in 1883 yet declared, "No one who has ever been upon it can forget it.") declared May 24 "The People's Day," an official Brooklyn holiday, and mounted flags in each of Brooklyn City Hall's 120 windows. New Yorkers, on the other hand, assumed the bridge would be a one-way street to Manhattan.

And later, the bittersweet wedding in 1898 when the bridge became a bride connecting the cities of Brooklyn to New York. To follow were the offspring of Williamsburg, Manhattan and the wayward Verrazano. In 1883, pundits predicted that over one hundred bridges would cross the East River a century later.

Genealogy dates the bridge's inception back to John Roebling, Washington's father, who had experimented with the Delaware Aqueduct, a suspension bridge for the Delaware & Hudson Canal and Gravity Rail Road to float barges from Pennsylvania down the Hudson to Brooklyn's Erie Basin, plus at least half a dozen other bridges. Other godfathers included James Stranahan, midwife of Prospect Park; Henry Cruse Murphy, founder of the *Brooklyn Eagle*; William Kingsley, *Eagle* editor; and Andrew Haskell Green, promoter of New York City unification.

When the Brooklyn toll booths opened at 11:20 p.m. (toll: one cent), everyone joined the festivities: H.D. VanKeuren paid the first toll; Mrs. C.G. Peck became the first woman to cross; and Charles Overton of Coney Island drove the first vehicle, a horse-powered wagon. The *New York Times* recorded the first beggar, the first drunk, the first policeman, the first hearse, the first "dude" and the first "negro." The first musician was a Scottish bagpiper among the 150,000 who crossed that day. Robert Odlum was the first to jump from the bridge (unsuccessfully); Steve Brodie never did. Paul Boyton, later of Coney Island and Sea Lion Park fame, attempted to rescue Odlum.

While the bridge was intended to replace the thirteen ferries, the last ferry line ran until 1942.

The heroine of the fairy tale, Emily Roebling, who transmitted her husband's missives to the workers for six years, died at fifty-nine. Her invalided husband outlived her to age eighty-nine, dying in 1926.

Then the spectacular centennial celebration in 1983 with more fireworks—this time by Grucci—and an interborough festival.

Here's to the Grand Old Lady! May she live to be one thousand!

All Things Brooklyn
February 24, 2012

Have you noticed how "Brooklyn" has slipped into being a trade name? The *Times* did a few months ago. Ran a feature story on how Manhattan clubs, pubs, foods and *tchotchkes* flaunt the "Brooklyn" label. In other words: Brooklyn sells.

Initially, the word evolved from "Breuckelen" into Brookland. Then a few other adaptations slipped in (Brockland, Brookline and Brocklin) before our burghers finally settled on Brooklyn. Whereas the word promoted local pride in its formative years, it instilled confusion and even fear in the twentieth century. The local dialect added to the chaos. Strangers became hopelessly entwined in the monotonous repetition of street names and the mangled syntax of the natives.

But the local charm was exported by our expatriates, who often transplanted the place name to new communities. Not only in America but also around the world. At the same time, population of the borough grew so that the county of Kings is the largest in New York State.

But as of the twenty-first century, popular opinion has changed. Brooklyn has developed an etymology and a Latin derivative: *brooklynensis* meaning "of or relating to Brooklyn." Suddenly, the name has become a cachet. In the popular media, characters named Brooklyn romp through the pages (and e-books) of children's literature. Then a Broadway musical with the abbreviated title *Bklyn* and a lead character named Brooklyn opened and stayed around awhile. Wasn't it bad enough that the hot dogs outside New York City are called coneys?

Now it is accepted as a proper female name, sometimes spelled "Brooklynn," "Brooklynne" or "Brooke Lynn." Not at all unusual. Other

Brooklyn, a Great Pyrenees, talking to Bandit, a Pomeranian. *Photo by John Manbeck.*

female place names are familiar; Brittany, Chelsea, Erin, Paris and Shannon come to mind, so why not Brooklyn? Online, a baby was christened Brooklyn Skye—two place names. According to the baby name website BabyHold, "Brooklyn" even has a meaning: water, stream.

Most consider Brooklyn a name for a girl, but David Beckham's son is named Brooklyn. Among girls, the name has broken the top one hundred since 2008, according to thinkbabynames.com. Even a Brooklyn Bridge popped up.

Of course, Borough President Marty Markowitz recognized the salability of the name when he invited supermodel Brooklyn Decker to his State of the Borough ceremony. Not that she's a native, but it's the name that counts. On the other hand, I read that she hails from Ohio (and North Carolina) and that she was named after a horse, Brook. It's just a touch of show business to add the suffix "lyn." She could have taken the name from a local dog, a three-year-old Great Pyrenees named Brooklyn. He loves the name as well as all this winter's snow.

Part II
CLASS AND CULTURE

Brooklyn Heights Association
March 4, 2010

Years ago, the Brooklyn Borough president's office compiled the celebratory book *The Brooklyn Century*. The twentieth century witnessed many memorable events, including the twenty-five-year tenure of Borough President Howard Golden not to mention several wars. But one of the most dominant events turned out to be the creation of the Brooklyn Heights Association (BHA), one of Brooklyn's oldest neighborhood associations.

Neighborhood associations, as opposed to homeowners' associations, have a distinctive difference with legal and financial ramifications. Dean Alvord developed Prospect Park South in 1892 on land purchased from the Flatbush Dutch Reformed Church. By 1905, the residents had established the Prospect Park South Neighborhood Association, which publishes a newsletter and maintains garden malls in the vicinity. Residents there promote a rivalry with the Heights, citing their large lawns and parking spaces. It still functions as the borough's oldest neighborhood association.

Although Brooklyn Heights antedated Prospect Park South to become Brooklyn's first suburb and first landmarked neighborhood, the Brooklyn Heights Association that formed in 1910 created an active presence that preserved the brownstone bedroom community. The presence of the many hotels indicated that Brooklyn Heights served as a hub of finance and commerce.

Postcard of Plymouth Church. *Author's collection.*

This year's centennial celebration opened on January 20 with a salute from Borough President Marty Markowitz and a film tribute composed of excerpts from major films shot on the streets of the Heights and hosted by director Peter Hedges. Included in the montage were scenes from *Without a Trace*, with backgrounds of older Montague, Remsen and Henry Streets; *Moonstruck*, with shots of Cranberry Street; *Burn After Reading*, with Middagh Street standing in for Washington's Georgetown; and *Catch Me If You Can*, with the Municipal Building substituting for Chase Manhattan Bank. Scenes from *The Sentinel* sparked gasps as realtor Ava Gardner at the end showed the modern high-rise that (in the film) replaced the mammoth Remsen Street mansion on the Promenade.

The highlight of every year remains the Landmark House and Garden Tour, an entrée to the private brownstones and frame houses of the Heights. Added to that this year will be a special exhibit at the Brooklyn Museum, a fall party at the Plymouth Church to celebrate the Brooklyn Bridge and a holiday pub and restaurant crawl.

The sylvan origins of the community atop the palisade attracted both farmers and wealthy landowners in 1636. With seven houses by the inlet and a utopian colony planned, the Dutch village of Breuckelen soon began to grow into a town and then the hub of a city. After the American Revolution, in which Brooklyn Heights played a strategic role, the City of Brooklyn evolved, grew and annexed surrounding towns. Hezekiah Pierrepont gridded streets of the Heights in 1820, memorializing local landowners in street names. The new Fulton Ferry evolved into a valuable development ally.

When the mid-century population increased, brownstones and sandstone houses joined the original clapboard houses while below the Heights, waterfront commerce thrived. With the growth of Brooklyn and New York, the construction of the Brooklyn Bridge guaranteed Brooklyn's future expansion—and the 1898 consolidation. With the merger, Brooklyn lost its independence and the Heights its glamour. To counter the slide, the BHA was founded in 1910 to preserve the condition of the streets and buildings of the neighborhood, seeing the intrusion of rail transportation both under and above it as a threat to its peace.

With the ascendancy of Robert Moses as transportation czar, the Heights was threatened again by a 1940s plan to build the proposed Brooklyn–Queens Expressway through Hicks and Henry Streets. Confronted by opposition, Moses decided to hang three decks from the palisade creating the Promenade surmounting three roadways.

In the 1960s, developers now threatened preservationists, as brownstones attracted a newer, younger population. The BHA persevered by creating New York City's first designated landmarked district in 1965. Over the years, the association took stands on the creation of Cadman Plaza, the height of new construction, the preservation of the Hotel St. George, rehabilitation of P.S. 8, care for the street trees in the Heights and the gardens along the Promenade, as well as the proposal for a park underneath it. A recent drive to replace streetlights on Montague Street stirred controversy.

The centennial events are presided over by Judy Stanton, executive director, and BHA president Tom van den Bout. The BHA website can be found at www.thebha.org.

Brooklyn Casinos
March 27, 2008

Today, the mention of the word "casino" causes an outburst. Sides form for and against gambling—those who think they have every right to get lucky, though they seldom do, against those who think it is morally reprehensible. Besides, it suggests lower-class activities.

Heights Casino in Brooklyn Heights. *Photo by John Manbeck.*

In the nineteenth century, a casino had diverse meanings, all of them pleasant and inviting. Generally, casino referred to a meeting hall used for dances or other entertainment. In Italy, the word meant a hunting lodge, although this reference could be deceiving—think Monte Cassino near Naples.

A notable casino exists in Brooklyn Heights today, yet no one thinks of gambling in the Heights Casino at 75 Montague Street, except for a personal wager on a squash or tennis match. (The Heights Casino, built in 1905, was preceded by the 1887 Brooklyn Heights Tennis Club at State and Smith Streets.)

No gambling was implied by the word "casino." In fact, the suspicion of gambling in Coney Island created a hearing in 1887 at which Paul Bauer, the owner of the West Brighton Hotel and Casino in Coney Island, testified that he never witnessed gambling at his casino:

> *Q: Did gambling go on in the rear room?*
> *A: Yes, sir.*

Q: How could you get to the back room?
A: Through a door.
Q: Did you ever see chips about any part of the room you owned?
A: No, sir.
Q: Did you state under oath that there never were chips about that room?
A: I never saw any chips.
Q: What are chips?
A: They are chips to play poker with.
Q: Have you ever played poker?
A: I have.
Q: And used the chips?
A: Yes, sir.
Q: Mr. Bauer, was there not about your establishment a man who sold chips and who went by the name of "The Professor?"
A: Oh, no, no, sir. You got that wrong.
Q: Who did you mean by speaking about the professor?
A: The professor is a big man, a book writer. He has got his family there, very respectable people.
Q: I am asking you about the people who were not respectable.
A: I ain't got any.

Bauer's casino introduced heavyweight boxing to Coney Island, a sport that was as illegal as gambling. By 1899, the hotel had burned down, but the casino, the Coney Island Athletic Club, still sponsored fights promoted by William Brady before he graduated to Broadway as a producer. Across from the Charlie Feltman's restaurants and hall was the Sea Beach Casino in the railroad terminal. And at the end of Ocean Parkway stood Reisenweber's Casino, a branch of a very respectable Manhattan restaurant.

By 1892, the *Brooklyn Daily Eagle* tried to define "casino" and decided that it was neither a music hall nor a theater, because stage sets were not allowed. On the other hand, the new Carnegie Hall was labeled a casino and featured Lillian Russell, who had just appeared at Brooklyn's Park Theater. She starred at Carnegie in a theatrical production described as "burlesque of the very highest quality."

Other high-toned casinos featured operas. Traveling around the cities were the Casino Opera Company and the New York Casino, which presented operettas. The Bennett Casino at Fulton Street and Alabama Avenue burned in 1894, but the Fifth Avenue Casino Company featured twenty bowling alleys and two billiard parlors.

Most casinos could be found in recreation areas near beaches. In 1900, the Bergen Casino in the Bergen Beach amusement park advertised "The Girl in Black" with "30 PEOPLE 30." Ulmer Park at Twenty-fifth Avenue in Gravesend used its casino for dances and entertainment until it burned down.

North of Ulmer Park was the Bath Beach Casino. Sheepshead Bay prided itself on McLoughlin's Bayside Casino next to its Bayside Hotel. The blocks are now occupied by the Lundy's building and the El Greco Diner.

So when you see a classic building with the word "casino" carved into its brick façade, don't look for slot machines—just get ready to party.

Religion in the City of Churches
March 9, 2006

When the Dutch traders arrived here, their religion arrived with them. Religion was very important at the time; wars still were fought over beliefs. Some of the bitterest struggles were fought between denominations of Protestants, not against other sects. The Thirty Years War—essentially against Catholicism—broke out over philosophies of the Puritans and the Calvinists, even though only slight differences emerged between their concepts of salvation.

The Dutch were largely Calvinists, but the Pilgrims in New England were Anglicans. While they welcomed thirty French Protestant Walloons in 1624, the Dutch established the Reformed Church in 1628. This was the official church of New Amsterdam, which reformed from Lutheranism but added the concept of free will. At least four Dutch Reformed churches still stand in Brooklyn.

New Netherland, however, was destined to be a trading post, not a colony. Peter Minuet, its first governor, never enforced the Dutch religion and disagreed openly with the pastor, Jonas Michaelius, perhaps because Minuet was a German and a Huguenot. One of Minuet's successors, Peter Stuyvesant, a military man, disagreed. He enforced the Dutch religion and even tried to prevent non-Dutch settlers from emigrating to the community. In 1654, he forbade twenty-three Sephardic Jews from Brazil to settle, but with some assistance from Jewish stockholders in the Dutch West India Company, the decision was reversed. On the whole, the Dutch merchants welcomed diversity and workers from any creed.

When the Dutch surrendered to the English, Governor Edmund Andros tried to replace the Dutch Reformed denomination with the Anglican. Then, after the American Revolution, official religions became a moot point, and Brooklyn emerged as the "City of Churches." In 1800, the African Methodist Episcopal Church, also known as Bridge Street Church and Zion Church, opened near the East River, the first African American church in Brooklyn.

Until the Irish immigration of the 1830s, New York was primarily English stock. The first foreign-speaking group to arrive in New York was the Germans, and by 1790, over 2,500 German Americans had settled in a community south of Manhattan's City Hall. By 1840, political difficulties between fiefdoms, as well as famine, oppression and unemployment, drove 24,000 more Germans here. When conditions became crowded, they moved to *Kleindeutschland* or *Deutschländle* on the lower East Side, popularly known as Dutchtown or Little Germany. As eastern European Jews moved in for linguistic association, many Germans moved up to Yorkville and over to Brooklyn's Eastern District, Williamsburg and Greenpoint. At the time, Germany was a divided country. Religiously, they were Calvinists, Lutherans, Catholics and Jews tied together by a common language. In reality, they were divided by dialects, politics and regional differences into Swabians, Bavarians, Hessians and Prussians. Philosophically, many were free thinkers influenced by the German Enlightenment.

A Century of Jehovah's Witnesses
April 29, 2010

A century ago, the Borough of Brooklyn sprang to life. In 1898, the City of Brooklyn morphed into the Borough of Brooklyn. While the borough no longer had the prestige of the "fourth largest city in America," it still retained a panache that captured the imagination. So the beginning of the twentieth century saw the organization of the Brooklyn Heights Neighborhood Association, the opening of the Brooklyn Museum, the founding of the Brooklyn Botanic Garden and the relocation of Jehovah's Witnesses headquarters from Pittsburgh to Brooklyn Heights. Now the Witnesses are moving to upstate New York, abandoning their very notable Brooklyn presence and property for more commercial interests.

The mark they left on Brooklyn is significant. As the Bible Student Association, they moved their headquarters to the Heights in 1909 and incorporated as the People's Pulpit Association. In 1942, the third president, Nathan Knorr, started buying Brooklyn real estate, moving their headquarters to 25 and 30 Columbia Heights.

Among their thirty Heights and Dumbo properties are many readily identifiable buildings. Their warehouse and shipping complex at 360 Furman Street moved upstate to Watchtower Farms in Walkill, so the fourteen-story building was sold in 2004 for $205 million (tax free), soon to emerge as One Brooklyn Bridge Park.

The Bossert, a former fourteen-story hotel at 98 Montague Street, has been on the market since 2008 but just sold. Opened the year the Witnesses moved to Brooklyn, the hotel was built on the site of the Pierrepont House by lumber tycoon Louis Bossert, who expanded it in 1914. While popular with transients and long-term residents (including the Brooklyn Dodgers), it fell out of favor in the 1970s. The Witnesses leased the building in 1983, purchasing it outright in 1988 and following with a full restoration of its Italian Renaissance Revival style. It will reopen again as a private hotel in 2013.

Another former hotel, the twelve-story Standish Arms at 169 Columbia Heights, built in 1903, was sold in 2007 by the Witnesses for $50 million and converted to luxury rentals as The Standish. After a disastrous fire in 1966, the hotel lost business until it was leased by the Witnesses in 1981 as a residential hotel for their members and then purchased in 1988. Numbers 161 and 183 Columbia Heights were sold as a package; three more at 165 Columbia Heights, 105 Willow Street and 34 Orange Street were sold privately.

The residence at 89 Hicks Street, built in 1940, has forty-eight units and was purchased by Brooklyn Law School in 2006 for $14 million. New York University, which recently merged with Brooklyn Polytech, acquired the twenty-six-floor "sliver building" at 67 Livingston Street in 2006 for $18.6 million. In place of the former Hotel Margaret (1889), which had burned to the ground in 1980, the Witnesses built an eleven-story modernistic office at 97 Columbia Heights in 1980 that looks out of place in Victorian Brooklyn Heights. They wanted to build it higher, but the Landmarks Preservation Commission wouldn't allow it.

The worldwide Watchtower Bible and Tract Society numbers over 7 million followers. Founded in 1876 by Charles Taze Russell as Bible Students, the organization followed an evangelistic fervor governed by a patriarchal leadership of elders. Moving to Brooklyn in 1909 enabled them to be near the waterfront and its shipping. The four-story brownstone at 124 Columbia Heights, formerly the parsonage of Henry Ward Beecher, became a residence for the staff. A Plymouth Church building at 13–17

Hicks Street became the Watchtower headquarters and auditorium, which they named Bethel. Their auditorium became the Brooklyn Tabernacle, but it was sold in 1918.

Acquisition of Brooklyn real estate continued with the purchase of 122 Columbia Heights in 1909 and construction of a new building on Furman Street in 1911. Other Witnesses properties in Brooklyn appeared on Myrtle, Concord, Adams and Sands Streets in the 1920s. In 1926, long before the historic designation of Brooklyn Heights, four brownstones on Columbia Heights were purchased and demolished to construct the executive offices and their Kingdom Hall. In 1931, Jehovah's Witnesses became the official name of the organization.

More realty on Columbia Heights was purchased in the 1940s and 1950s, and two residential buildings rose there at 107 and at 119 in 1969. Further expansion in 1969 included the purchase of the Squibb complex and, a few years later, the Towers. Many of the properties are connected by underground tunnels.

While these facilities accommodate the 70,000 national and international visitors annually (who speak 440 languages), the existence of the Witnesses has not been without controversy. They use their own translation of the Bible called the *New World Translation of the Holy Scriptures*, which predicts that Armageddon will destroy the world, allowing only 144,000 people into Heaven. Predictions for the end of the world have been issued for 1914, 1925 and 1975, to no avail. Witnesses don't vote, salute any flag or serve in the military. They don't accept blood transfusions, and they refuse to observe Christmas, Easter or birthdays on the grounds that they are based on pagan rituals. All of this causes trouble, yet among their followers have been or are President Dwight Eisenhower; the Williams sisters, Venus and Serena; Prince, the singer; George Benson, the jazz guitarist; the Jackson Five; the Wayans Brothers; and Mickey Spillane, the writer.

So, after a century here in Brooklyn, the Witnesses are slowly leaving the First Suburb, Brooklyn Heights, for the upstate suburbs of Patterson, New York, where they will build their headquarters, an educational center and their bethel on 240 acres. The property there, which they started purchasing in the 1960s and continued into the 1970s and '80s, includes their latest Ramapo purchase, a 2009 addition that cost $11.5 million.

But moving that many people and divesting all their Brooklyn property will not happen overnight. So expect to be greeted by the friendly Witnesses for several more years, just as Truman Capote had encountered them on Willow Street in the 1940s.

Part III
SPORTS

Once There Was a Ballpark
March 25, 2008

Many years ago, Brooklyn had its very own Major League Baseball team called the Dodgers. You may have heard of them.

In 1955, Walter O'Malley, president of the Brooklyn Dodgers, complained that the team had outgrown Ebbets Field, so he sold the park to Marvin Kratter with the intention of leasing it back for the next three years. He wanted a new domed ballpark, which he thought would be fine at Atlantic and Flatbush Avenues. Then the team left to play exhibition games in Japan.

Brooklyn Borough President John Cashmore approved of the planned new park, but New York City Parks Commissioner Robert Moses did not. Moses said he did not want public money involved. Imagine that! So he planned for a federally funded housing project on O'Malley's proposed stadium site. He said that the stadium would look fine atop the Atlantic Avenue Long Island Rail Road (LIRR) station, to be financed through a bond issue from the Sports Authority. Then he chastised O'Malley for even thinking of using public money and the city's power of eminent domain to build a sports stadium to make himself rich. Moses said, "Walter honestly believes that he in himself constitutes a public purpose." The Board of Estimate, the city's funding agency, agreed with Moses. O'Malley then made phone calls to Los Angeles.

But L.A. did not have any more of a stadium than Brooklyn did. Mayor Robert Wagner, concerned that the city was losing two baseball teams (the New York Giants as well as the Brooklyn Dodgers) tried to mend fences. Moses offered to build a Dodgers stadium in Flushing Meadows, Queens, at parks department expense. If O'Malley didn't accept, he concluded, "It won't happen."

Moses was right. The estimate on the proposed stadium and land was revealed to be $20.7 million. But Los Angeles was more accommodating. They were willing to propose a stadium site on land in the Chavez Ravine that had been designated to be public housing for poor Mexicans.

O'Malley countered Moses by offering to buy the Atlantic Avenue site if the city would condemn the land, which was filled with "slums," according to Doris Kearns Goodwin. Meanwhile, on the West Coast, the ante offered was three hundred acres of the ravine plus $4 million for preparation. O'Malley would pay $10 million for the stadium.

The New York City Board of Estimate never reacted. They refused to condemn the Atlantic Avenue land and hesitated to authorize a $30 million stadium.

In October 1957, O'Malley flew to Los Angeles with a contract for his Dodgers. After several ugly scenes in which people were evicted, Dodgers Stadium opened in 1962. Two years later, Shea Stadium opened in Flushing Meadows.

Baseball, of course, returned to Brooklyn in a truncated form in 2001. Fostered by a mayor who drove to have two farm teams in the city no matter what the cost, the Cyclones opened in Coney Island's Keyspan Park. It was a dream that O'Malley could only wish for. Not only did the city pick up all the expenses but it also built on a city park property taken over when Fred Trump defaulted on Steeplechase land. The only condemnation was of the Thunderbolt, a privately owned roller coaster relic of historic Coney Island. The winner was Fred Wilpon, the Cyclone team owner, and the people of Brooklyn (although they lost, too).

So Brooklyn is having a renaissance, a rebirth of its better days. Risky neighborhoods are being gentrified, gourmet chefs have commandeered key communities, condos are replacing parking lots and even our prison has closed for lack of business. Now we have new developers and politicians to fill in for the Moses and the O'Malley of yesteryear. Their names are Ratner, Wilpon and Pataki. The scenario hasn't changed much. They all want the same results: big profits at the expense of the taxpayers.

In the nineteenth century, owners of railroads had their own bag of tricks to "condemn" land. Courts closed on weekends, so railroad condemnations started on Friday night. Once rails crossed private land, the railroads had the right of way, which—when courts opened on Monday—was recognized. After all, even private railroads were a public convenience.

Mayor Rudy Giuliani understood this when he ordered the Thunderbolt demolished on a Friday night, and Robert Moses understood this when he confiscated Long Island farms and Brooklyn neighborhoods for his beloved highways. Now we have the Nets coming to the same neighborhood that O'Malley desired, which also happens to involve a railroad: the MTA-owned Long Island Rail Road. The winner gets not only an arena but also the confiscated land that goes with it—at taxpayer expense. When it comes to eminent domain and construction of stadiums and railroads, a lot of little eggs must be broken.

Brooklyn's Baseball Myth
June 24, 2002

Baseball has long been fantasized as the king of Brooklyn sports. Remember the Brooklyn Dodgers? Dream on.

As of 2002, the longevity of the Dodgers in Tinsel Town has been double its Brooklyn life span. Yet the die-hard Brooklyn fans have cited the name Dodgers, with its fabled history of fans dodging trolley cars to get to the ballpark. (Not even Ebbets Field.) "Why should the team be allowed to keep the name Dodgers?" they argue. "No trolleys out in Los Angeles," they say.

Wrong again! L.A. had one of the most extensive trolley networks in the country, albeit before the Dodgers moved there. Remember the movie *Who Framed Roger Rabbit?*

But Brooklynites were lucky to have kept baseball in the hometown at all. Within several years of their founding, the owner struck a deal with Baltimore to move them to Maryland as the Orioles. But Charlie Ebbets saved the day and bought the team for Brooklyn.

Well how about those loyal Flatbush fans? First of all, Ebbets Field was in Crown Heights, just across the city boundary from Flatbush. In a pinch, how loyal were those fans? No way! They stayed home, listening to Red Barber describe the games on radio. No TV then. At average games, they became as rare as fans that showed up for the invisible Brooklyn *football* Dodgers.

Attendance slipped to an all time low—until the evil O'Malley pulled the plug. Then everybody got upset. Leave it to the politicians—Borough

Night game with the Cyclones. *Photo by John Manbeck.*

President John Cashmore and New York City Parks Commissioner Robert Moses—to argue and delay a decision over the proposed Atlantic Avenue site until the team had boarded the train west. Moses wanted to move the Dodgers to the former fairgrounds in Queens! (Eventually, the deed happened—only they were called the Mets.)

Still, the Bums pulled off an almost win in the World Series and a definite win in their last "home" game against Pittsburgh. The Borough of Brooklyn lost one of the most colorful teams in baseball history, but the hometown natives didn't even know it until they were long gone. Now they cry!

Thanks to Giuliani's generosity, professional baseball has returned to Brooklyn with the Cyclones. It's nice—really nice—even though the ex-mayor ripped off the city and the public in ways Charlie Ebbets never dreamed of. With the amount of money contributed by the city to build Keyspan Park (now MCU Park), admission should be free. We already paid our entrance fee with our taxes. Add to the entrance price the overpriced beer and ice cream and souvenirs. And compound that with ads wherever you look.

But the size of the ballpark is just right. Ebbets would have approved. I always get vertigo in those other coliseums. And the location of Keyspan guarantees a pleasant summer evening—unless it rains. But minor league players present another baseball problem. Unlike major league players, they're not around from season to season. Where are the Reeses, Robinsons and Sniders to root for? Each year, we must get to know new rookies. If they're still around for the new season, we ask, "What's wrong with them?" They're an enthusiastic bunch of players, and this scale of baseball is just right for the time. Why? Because Brooklyn STILL can't support a major-league team, no matter how much we fantasize.

Baseball is not Brooklyn's sport. It hasn't been since baseball switched from a participatory sport to a spectator farrago. The only baseball that fans are enthusiastic about is that played in the Parade Ground. We have so many new immigrants who aren't familiar with the roots of our love affair with baseball. Why should they care?

Basketball is a better contender for a Brooklyn sport. Pickup games are more readily available than grouping eighteen players around a baseball diamond. Maybe they could be called the Brooklyn Nets.

Handball still reigns in certain Brooklyn neighborhoods, and bocce claims loyalty in others. Even tennis and golf have gained respectable followings, but sadly, these too have been transformed into spectator sports. Among the tykes, there's soccer, with an increase of girls' teams. Maybe it's a more democratic activity. Soccer little leagues outnumber baseball teams. With the Caribbeans, there's cricket. Can rugby be far apart? How about lacrosse and polo? What's more, these activities have longer seasons and demand a greater attention span than baseball does. Only during a World Series do baseball fans become rabid. Just like the Super Bowl. Where are these fans the rest of the year? These extravaganzas become excuses for commercial food orgies.

No, Brooklyn was a sporting town, but only when baseball was so new that virtually anyone could play on a local team.

The really big spectator sport in Brooklyn was horse racing at Sheepshead, Brighton and Gravesend. But that's a horse of a different color.

Brooklyn's Grand Marathon
November 5, 2009

While the annual New York City Marathon usually faces pleasant weather, the Brooklyn Marathon in 1909—a century ago—prepared Brooklynites for

Spectators watch the Brooklyn Marathon, 1909. *Library of Congress.*

James Clarke, winner of the 1909 Brooklyn Marathon. *Library of Congress.*

any possible threatening climatic challenges. Started the previous year, the race tried the endurance of the 150 runners because it was run on Lincoln's Birthday, February 12. The runners started at the Thirteenth Armory in Crown Heights, ran along Ocean Parkway, then past Coney Island's silent amusements to Sea Gate and back, a twenty-six-mile run. In 1909, the temperatures dipped to the thirties, as can be attested by the 250,000 fans seen wearing overcoats in photos from the event.

After the race, fan favorite James Crowley posed with the warmly dressed spectators. Crowley, a member of the Irish-American Athletic Club, was known as "King of the Marathoners" because he had finished more marathons than anyone else. The year before he had won the Yonkers Marathon on Thanksgiving Day before a crowd of twenty thousand. Later, in December 1908, he finished second in the marathon from Rye to Columbus Circle, Manhattan. By 1910, Crowley hit his stride again by breaking all records at Celtic Park, Queens.

Unfortunately, Crowley came in second in the 1909 Brooklyn Marathon, losing to James Clarke. Crowley entered the Boston Marathon later the same year but came in fourth up in Beantown. Possibly, it was because Crowley was barefoot, while Clarke wore garters on his stockings. Edwin White came in fifth.

A second twenty-six-mile Brooklyn Marathon took place the following week, February 22, Washington's Birthday, with one hundred runners starting. Using a similar route, Clarke was the favorite. (Crowley opted out on this one.) Clarke started ahead of the pack but began to fail at mile twenty-two, according to the *New York Times*. The race finished in the Armory with several turns around the inside track with Clarke hopelessly trying to catch up. He came in third, with Albert Raines of the Xavier Athletic Association coming in second. The winner? Edwin White of Holy Cross Lyceum!

The route of this Brooklyn Marathon started at the Armory to Prospect Park West to Grand Army Plaza; then from Albany Avenue to Clarkson to Flatbush to Cortelyou to Ocean Parkway; finally from Surf Avenue to West Thirty-first Street. They returned from Surf to Ocean Parkway to Parkside, then from Ocean Avenue to Flatbush to Prospect Park West, finishing at the Armory.

The Brooklyn Marathon continued until 1915. By then, February temperatures had dropped to zero, so the wiser minds cancelled it.

A modified fifteen-mile version of the Brooklyn race took place in Coney Island in 1922. In 1928, a marathon sponsored by *Il Progresso*, the Italian newspaper, started at Elm Street in Manhattan and finished at the Luna Park amusement center in Coney Island. That race was marked by runner-automobile collisions and several major injuries. In other races, spectators often joined the competition.

But the serious runners had to wait until 1970, when the five-borough New York Marathon was founded. The Cherry Tree Marathon (on Washington's Birthday, with blizzard dangers), established in 1959, preceded today's marathon. It ran through Bronx streets and finished near Yankee Stadium. The first New York City Marathon restricted itself to Central Park, with four loops around the roadways. In 1973, the event attracted sponsors. The race was routed through all five boroughs in 1976 in honor of the country's bicentennial. By 1981, the competition earned media status, with the race being televised.

Today's marathon races date back to the first modern one held in 1896, a twenty-five-mile race between Athens and Marathon, Greece. Boston started their marathon race in 1897, still the oldest continuous one being run. In the New York vicinity, Yonkers began one in 1907 held in November. A marathon in December 1908 started in the Bronx and passed through Harlem to a finale at Columbus Circle. Another marathon in 1909 was held at the old Madison Square Garden (Madison Square at Twenty-third Street), and a "marathon derby" took place at the Polo Grounds that same year.

With an American winner, Meb Keflezighi, in 2009, as well as six Americans finishing in the top ten, the marathon has again become an American sport after twenty-seven years of natives losing out. The fortieth New York City Marathon has become an event New Yorkers are proud of. It's just too bad the winner lives in California, not Brooklyn.

The Great Black Hope
February 24, 2005

"The Great White Hope," a saga about fervent but bigoted passions to defeat heavyweight Jack Johnson, was the plot of *Incredible Blackness*, the documentary by Ken Burns shown on PBS.

Johnson's story had the drama of race, sex and money during a time when bigotry rampantly disgraced America. Johnson, in many ways, loomed bigger than life. He appeared in Brooklyn at least once, not in the boxing ring but at the Sheepshead Bay Speedway, racing a car. But earlier, in 1890, a more positive success story unwound at the same track when horses thundered down the turf there and Isaac Burns Murphy, a black jockey, starred in his own personal drama.

Jockey Isaac Murphy. *Library of Congress.*

Murphy, also known as "Ike" or the "Black Irishman," basked in waves of cheers from forty thousand fans rather than the ridicule and taunts that faced Johnson. By the time Murphy raced in Brooklyn, he was already a superhero, having won two Kentucky Derbies in 1884 and 1890. He would go on to win again in 1891, a record broken only in 1948 by Eddie Arcaro.

In the early days of racing, most jockeys were black. The sport had been a favorite in the South, where jockeys had been slaves. Southern businessmen introduced it in Saratoga, New York. Until the money incentive arose and the Ku Klux Klan appeared in the 1920s, white jockeys—such as Tod Sloan and Edward "Snapper" Garrison—were in the minority.

Betting on horses had been outlawed in New York, although wagers were surreptitiously placed at private tracks along Brooklyn's Ocean Parkway. Horse owners Leonard Jerome and August Belmont convinced supervisor John Y. McKane, Gravesend's political boss, to allow betting at the three tracks in his independent town: Sheepshead Bay, Brighton Beach and Gravesend. Their precedent had been the track at Saratoga, where high society socialized at the track. With his political clout in Albany, McKane successfully had the anti-betting legislation rescinded, and the social setting reappeared in Brooklyn.

Born to Isaac Burns on April 16, 1861, Murphy was a son of a slave who died in a Civil War prison camp. Adopted by his grandfather, Green Murphy, he took his grandfather's name. As a child, Isaac Murphy worked as an exercise boy for racetracks, but by fourteen, he had won his first race in 1878 on Falsetto. He went on to win every year for fifteen seasons.

Known for his kindness to horses (he never used a whip or spurs), Murphy developed a style of holding back until the final spurt. He was respected

Matched race at Sheepshead Bay Race Track between Salvatore and Tenny. *Library of Congress.*

for his honesty; he never wagered and refused bribes to throw races. For this, Murphy was well paid. In 1882, he earned $10,000 a year plus $25 for each win, "four times the salary of a U.S. senator and better than most statesmen," wrote the *Louisville Courier Journal* at his death. The newspaper named him "one of the greatest athletes of the nineteenth century," showing a "marvelous exhibition of courage, audacity and skill."

Murphy's Brooklyn race record became the talk of racing circles. The Sheepshead Bay track created The Futurity, a match race in which three-year-olds compete by their pedigrees and are matched before their births. On June 25, 1890, the match race was between Salvatore, ridden by Ike Murphy, and Tenny, ridden by Snapper Garrison, a popular Irish jockey. Salvatore won by a nose.

Murphy went on to win the American Derby four times and the Latonia Derby five times. His 44 percent win record remains unmatched. In his lifetime, he rode 628 winners in 1,412 races. He was so successful that in 1892 he retired from racing to his horse farm, where he owned and trained his own horses. When he died on February 12, 1896, at the age of thirty-six, he owned an estate worth $50,000.

Success brought problems, though. At his peak, Murphy weighed ninety-one pounds, and the high life that came with his victories caused him to become overweight. In addition, he faced alcoholism, which contributed to his death from anorexia and pneumonia.

Respected by his friends and peers, his Lexington, Kentucky Masonic funeral service included other famous black jockeys and trainers, Willie Sims and Tony Hamilton among them. "The casket is certainly the handsomest ever used in the burial of a colored man in Kentucky," wrote the *Courier Journal*. And Murphy was buried in the colored cemetery.

In 1955, Murphy became the first jockey elected to the National Museum of Racing and Hall of Fame in Saratoga. Then, in 1977, his body was reinterred in Kentucky Horse Park next to the body of the famous Man o' War. Ike Murphy had finally received the recognition he deserved.

Sammy Davis Jr. attempted to film a biopic of Murphy's life, but it never got off the ground. However, in 2003, John Taylor from Lexington completed a thirty-minute filmed tribute to the "Great Black Hope."

Brooklyn Wheelmen
April 14, 2005

Spring introduces flowers, encourages dieting and prompts us to tune up our bicycles. These two-wheeled vehicles became a form of mass transportation for nineteenth-century Brooklyn and introduced a new terminology: Brooklyn wheelmen. These bicyclists so loved the smooth, flat avenues of Kings County that they called it "Wheelmen's Paradise." Bedford Avenue was the best thoroughfare because it ran for eight miles, the length of Brooklyn.

Interest in bicycling grew with the new Victorian interest for other sports such as tennis, roller-skating and baseball. The wooden "bone shaker penny farthing" two-wheeler started the trend in the 1860s, and the first bicycle factory opened in 1872. Because of the sudden popularity, the word "bicycle" was used as a sound bite that referred to the new speed. The Boynton Bicycle Railroad was actually a monorail with single rows of seats as a bicycle has. It sped between New Utrecht (Bensonhurst) and Coney Island. The seat arrangement and speed justified the term "bicycle."

The Philadelphia Centennial, a world's fair to celebrate the founding of America, introduced the metal high-wheeled version of the bicycle in 1876. By 1881, the League of American Wheelmen was formed in Brooklyn. In the 1890s, the safety bicycle appeared with two equal-sized wheels that allowed the vehicle to assume a more practical use.

Bicycle clubs, a new development, built bicycles for multiple riders, similar to a stretch limo. The Germania Club constructed one for ten riders. The *Brooklyn Eagle* founded the Brooklyn Municipal Club, which sponsored bicycle trips. Among the rich, a triplet was popular, with a professional driver pedaling from the third seat. "Diamond Jim" Brady gave a triplet to his friend, Lillian Russell, with the diamond initials L.R. embedded on the frame. Since the combined weight of the couple was over five hundred pounds, it may be assumed that the professional driver earned his salary.

Of course, once a new activity is popularized, others find fault and dangers. The dress of the cyclists created a new fashion movement—but not without repercussions. Clergymen voiced complaints about the risqué bicycle clothing women wore, called bloomers. They also objected to cyclists riding past their church doors on Sunday.

Bicycle parades surged in popularity, with musicians playing their instruments while riding in military formation. In 1895, the Ocean Parkway Bicycle Path, newly macadamized, opened with musical fanfare. Manhattan Beach Hotel created its own bicycle racetrack around the same time. Theodore Roosevelt, while New York City police commissioner, introduced a bicycle platoon within the police corps.

During the Great Depression, the more practical street cycle, with balloon tires, appeared, but World War II, with its rationing of rubber and metal, halted production for the duration of the war. After the war, Schwinn introduced the Cadillac of bicycles with its chrome and front-spring suspension. Then, English racing bikes such as Raleighs led the drive for multi-speed vehicles.

New York City Parks Commissioner Robert Moses contracted for a citywide bicycle path system with access at Shore Parkway to Long Island. More recently, this bikeway has been expanded to a Greenway System running 150 miles through the city. Mayor Bloomberg has promised a greenway around Manhattan.

Brooklyn's Prospect Park has been closed to automotive traffic in summers and on weekends. Now bicycling has taken on such importance that city streets are closed for bike rides in the spring and fall. Bike New York attracts twenty thousand cyclists who ride through the five boroughs in the spring.

Bicycle parade, 1896. *Brooklyn Public Library, Brooklyn Collection.*

In the fall, the New York City Century, a one-hundred-mile bicycle event, attracts several thousand participants. Critical Mass, a renegade monthly bicycle event held on Fridays, has aroused police concern and a judicial response. The authorities still need to cope with this issue.

By far the most unusual bicycle tour is one given annually by Dr. Kenneth Jackson of Columbia University's history department. He leads a bicycle tour of historic New York City starting in Harlem at 11:00 p.m. The tour ends in Brooklyn Heights at 5:00 a.m. in front of the Plymouth Church with a re-creation of Henry Ward Beecher's abolitionist slave auction. It attracts a capacity crowd of over two hundred cyclists.

The Red Ball Trolleys
January 31, 2008

"The Red Ball Is Up Today" screamed the *Brooklyn Eagle*'s forty-five-point headline in 1895. That meant excitement for all. The red ball appeared on flags hung at Grand Army Plaza and on the front of trolley cars rattling

Crowds ice skating at Prospect Park, 1934. *Photo by Walter Henley.*

down Flatbush Avenue and throughout Brooklyn. The red ball announced that the ice on Prospect Park's lakes was at least four inches thick and safe for ice skating. Long before the Wollman Ice Skating Rink, Brooklynites anticipated the joy of skating in Prospect Park. "It is probable that 7,000 of them used the ice during the afternoon," a reporter wrote. The *Eagle* files reveal that reporters described the skating activities enthusiastically.

From their offices in Litchfield Mansion, the park police diligently watched for inappropriate behavior. Occasionally, they arrested disorderly skaters or rescued skaters who fell through thin ice. Sometimes the public complained that the ice was not cleared of snow fast enough.

One story cited a man who was pushing his girl in a sleigh colliding with a busy figure skater concentrating on his moves. This resulted in the skater landing on the girl's lap and both of them falling on the ice. It "looked like love at first sight," the reporter commented. But then the skater flew away over the ice.

Another incident involved an Englishman with "amber hair" who bullied his way onto the ice, but then "his eyes began to pop, his mouth opened like that of a codfish…his fingers clutched the air…his skates shot eight feet high, and he landed on the crown of his high hat."

The thrill of skating on a brisk winter night appeared to be unmatched for our nineteenth-century forebears. "Of all the winter amusements, surely skating is the healthiest, the pleasantest, the most invigorating…*au natural*," which suggests that artificial ice would not do. Among its virtues, skating in Prospect Park "strengthens the body, broadens the mind, improves the temper, sharpens the appetite, adds grace to bodily movements, and even gives a fresh zeal to love."

Usually only the smaller lake was safe enough for skating, but after a particularly cold spell, even the larger lake froze over safely. Police limited the crowds, if necessary. Afternoons drew the biggest crowds, but office workers could skate at night under electric and kerosene lamps. Roaming peddlers sold pies, soft drinks, candy and cigarettes. A stand by the lake rented skates and offered hot coffee, chocolate and cider.

Private Walter Henley ice skating at Prospect Park in 1918. *Author's collection.*

Most skaters brought their own equipment, but ice chairs on runners could be leased, too. In 1880, a competition between ice boating clubs sparked an interest. The first official toboggan hill appeared in 1886.

But skaters drew the most attention, particularly when a skating carnival opened off Duck Island. An audience of ten thousand gathered to enjoy it. The carnival featured exhibition skating (by a Canadian) and a skating contest with varying levels of expertise: plain, roll and fancy figures. In 1893, Swedish skaters gave a strong performance, impressing the crowd. The winning female skater was Mrs. A.F. Cook. William Fitzsimmons won the men's skating medal.

The park commissioner presented a watch to a policeman who saved a man after he had fallen through the ice. Park police, who had to contend with crowds in winter and summer, games and an occasional suicide, were derided by city police. In 1889, a policeman earned $15 a week, while his pension amounted to $750 a year. At the same time, a salesman earned between $5 and $10 a week.

One writer reminisced about walking across the East River in the winter of 1866 and skating in the incomplete Prospect Par before it officially opened. He also noted that he had skated on a pond at Court Street and Hamilton Avenue in 1837. This skater also frequented Washington Pond (in today's Washington/James J. Byrne Park), Union Skating Pond and the Capitoline Skating and Ball Park.

Prospect Park replaced those skating ponds and rinks while providing warm winter fun when the weather outside was *frightfully* cold—cold enough to freeze the lake with four inches of ice.

The Hotel St. George Pool
July 16, 2009

Recent cries of "Foul!" have circled the preservationist blogs chastising Eastern Athletic for the demolition of the remainder of the murals surrounding the pool in the former Hotel St. George. While the marquee remains, although it is not the original entrance, not much of the old Brooklyn Heights landmark hotel is recognizable these days. Strangers must think that St. George is the name of the subway line that runs beneath.

The pool under the hotel opened in 1933 with water supplied by "natural artesian saltwater wells." Admission charges between $0.95 cents and $1.25 made it possible even for Depression-age children to swim there. Bathing suits, towels and use of the gym were included in the admission price. A mosaic design of aquatic scenes, interrupted by mirrors, surrounded the 40- by 120-foot pool, and an observation deck hung above the swimmers.

At the deep end stood a ten-foot diving board abutted by three lower boards. At the shallow end, a waterfall splashed into the pool. The mirrored ceiling reflected aquatic antics, making swimmers feel like Esther Williams or Johnny Weismuller. Construction of the pool cost $3.5 million. Neighbor Truman Capote swam there for relaxation. As a result of declining revenues, though, the pool, along with half of the rooms, closed in 1974.

The Hotel St. George had been the pride of Brooklyn as well as the largest hotel in all of New York City. Red-coated, white-gloved bellhops greeted guests at the Clark Street entrance, and over one thousand full-time employees waited on them. The lobby leading to the subway elevators contained shops similar to the ones today. That subway entrance, once the hotel's pride, sped guests from Times Square to Brooklyn in fifteen minutes.

Saltwater swimming pool at Hotel St. George. *Author's collection.*

Created in 1885 by former U.S. Navy captain William Tumbridge, the original ten-story, red brick hotel was designed by Augustus Hatfield. In 1890, Tumbridge added another structure with a roof deck surrounded by flagpoles. Tumbridge, who died in 1921, never envisioned the hotel's subsequent growth that started in 1928. Sections added then included the Colorama Ballroom (the largest banquet room in the world at that time), where hundreds of colored lights changed constantly; the pool; small apartments; and rooftop dining and dancing. A roof beacon beamed from the thirty-story St. George Tower. By 1931, the hotel boasted 2,632 rooms.

Within the hotel were the Drugstore-O-Rama, on the corner where a liquor store now stands; a coffee shop; and, on Pineapple Street, the St. George Playhouse. Across from the hotel on the corner of Clark and Henry Streets stood a Fanny Farmer candy store, while farther down Henry Street was the posh Patricia Murphy's Candlelight Restaurant.

So important was the Hotel St. George that a "Hotel St. George March" was written in 1925 while Brooklyn and Manhattan celebrities, debutantes, athletes and presidential candidates flocked there for events. Presidents Roosevelt and Truman spent nights at the St. George on separate occasions, while Lyndon Johnson stopped by for an event. The hotel catered to both transients and permanent guests. Brooklyn Bridge's fiftieth anniversary

Ad for Hotel St. George pool. *Author's collection.*

dinner was celebrated at the hotel in 1933 where New York City Mayor John O'Brien and Governor Alfred E. Smith honored the Roeblings. In 1946 and 1947, the Brooklyn Dodgers owned a suite of rooms at the St. George.

While finances declined in the Depression years, they spruced up during World War II, when U.S. Navy personnel spilled over from the Navy Yard. In 1957, Leonard Bernstein conducted a recording of the New York Philharmonic in the ballroom. Families of Korean War soldiers stayed there, and a scene from *The Godfather* was filmed in the hotel bar.

By the 1970s, further decline set in at the hotel and in Brooklyn Heights. The Tower suites became condos. A topless club, Wild Fyre, opened in the hotel. Homeless as well as AIDS and HIV patients were boarded in its rooms. In short, it became a single-room-occupancy (SRO) hotel.

Then, during the hot, dry summer of 1995, a disastrous sixteen-alarm fire raged throughout the "fireproof" building. (That merely meant exterior fire escapes were provided.) The damage caused by the fire has been repaired, and the original hotel has been divided into several parcels. Students board in one section, while an exclusive entrance on Clark Street caters to a new, richer clientele.

Down near Hicks Street, the Eastern Athletic Club took over the old Hotel St. George pool, transforming it into a kiddie pool and removing the remaining mosaic for "safety reasons."

Part IV

YOU GOTTA HAVE PARK

Back to Our Roots at Washington Park
May 15, 2008

Brooklyn's newest park may also be one of its oldest. J.J. Byrne Park is transforming back into Washington Park, although the Byrne name will be retained by the playground.

Washington, the father of our nation, had his name bestowed on towns, cities, states, parks, streets and babies in his honor. Similar acts of reverence occurred for John Kennedy and Martin Luther King.

Then, as several generations passed, the fealty was removed. So it was with Fort Greene, which started as Fort Putnam in 1812, whose construction was supervised by General Nathanael Greene. By 1815, the fort was decommissioned. Promoted by Walt Whitman from his perch in the *Brooklyn Eagle*, it changed into Washington Park in 1847, Brooklyn's first public park. Then Olmsted and Vaux, of Prospect Park fame, designed a new park in 1896. With the Martyrs' Monument added in 1908, Washington lost favor, and Fort Greene won. (On a tiny corner, his name remains with Washington Park Street.) Which brings us to Brooklyn's second Washington Park.

In 1883, a group of Brooklyn businessmen led by Charles Byrnes bought the Camden (New Jersey) Merritts, a baseball team in the Interstate League. They then leased a plot of land from the Litchfields (who owned most of South Brooklyn) for $30,000. Their grandstand had room for 2,500. At the opener on May 12, 1883, 6,000 came out to the ballgame at Washington Park to watch the Brooklyn Merritts beat Trenton, 12–6. Next year, the team moved to the American Association League.

The teams that played there were known as the Brooks, the Atlantics, the Bridegrooms, the Superbas and the Robins. They were all the same team, but not until 1933 were they officially the Dodgers. The Old Stone House, infamous from the Battle of Brooklyn, became the team's dugout.

The Washington Park grandstand was enlarged but still had a standing-room-only crowd on April 30. Then tragedy struck in 1899, when the team was on the road. A discarded lit cigar started a fire that destroyed the new grandstand. As the Brooklyn Atlantics, the team moved to Ridgewood, Queens, and in 1891 to Eastern Park in East New York.

With Washington Park rebuilt, the Brooklyn team returned to make baseball history. The new park had its entrance on Fourth Avenue and Third Street, and the new team built its glory with colorful heroes. The starting pitcher in 1898, Brickyard Kennedy, lived up to his name. Hughie Jennings joined the lineup in 1899. Their biggest nemesis, the Giants, brought in their "boy wonder from Bucknell," Christy Mathewson, who walloped Brooklyn every time. But they still won the National League pennant in 1899 and 1900.

The biggest challenge was not a team but Sunday blue laws, which prohibited paid amusement on a Sunday. In 1904, Judge William Gaynor (later mayor of New York) ruled in favor of Brooklyn, but the following year, police arrested the entire team. In 1908, Charlie Ebbets began looking for space for a new ballpark.

In 1909, Zack Wheat, an American Indian, joined the Superbas, and Casey Stengel signed up in 1912. On opening day, April 11, 1912, a crowd of thirty thousand watched the Giants run up the score 18–3 before the game was called because of darkness. This last year for Washington Park also saw the Superbas lose the last game to the Giants, 1–0. The next year, the team premiered at the new Ebbets Field.

When the Superbas moved out of Washington Park, Robert Ward's Tip Tops of the Federal League moved in. (Ward baked Tip Top Bread.) But then the Federal League folded, and the park remained empty until 1918, when the federal government used it as a storehouse for war supplies. Eventually, the grandstand and dugout were demolished in 1926 when Con Edison bought the property. Only a wall remains on Third Avenue.

Meanwhile, James J. Byrne was serving as the chief clerk at the Bureau of Public Buildings. In 1907, he was appointed as the commissioner of

Waiting for the gates to open at Washington Park. *Library of Congress.*

public works. In September 1926, Borough President Joseph Guider died in office. James Byrne was selected to fill Guider's term, becoming Brooklyn's ninth borough president. Among his good deeds was his ordering that the Old Stone House be rebuilt and commissioning the Municipal Building on Joralemon Street and the Central Court Building on Schermerhorn Street. These accomplishments were enough for Byrne to be elected to his own term of office in 1929, not a very propitious year. The next year, Byrne too died in office and was replaced by Henry Hesterberg.

Washington's name had begun to fade from history when the parks department acquired three acres on the Park Slope/Sunset Park border in 1926. To honor the Brooklyn executive who had restored the Old Stone House (as a storage shed with rest rooms), the parks department renamed the former Washington Park for J.J. Byrne in 1933.

Fast forward to 2008. Kim Maier, the director of the Old Stone House, recommended the restoration of the name "Washington Park." The late Herb Yellin, a founder of the First Battle Alliance, had supported the name change years ago. As Brooklyn Borough Historian, I thought it was only just. On March 12, 2008, Community Board 6 agreed and voted the deed done.

The Marine Park Dream
March 22, 2007

Brooklyn Bridge Park is facing reality! Preliminary cleanup is underway, and the dream will form beneath our Promenade. Just as last summer's Floating Pool fascinated Brooklynites, construction of the new park will captivate us for years. Constructing a park is not just visualizing a dream; it takes years of planning and work. The planning phase is over. Now the labor begins.

Prospect Park, our green refuge in central Brooklyn, had its hills and lakes and forests created before the Picnic House, Boat House and statuary materialized. The result, with its boulevards projecting east and south, created grandeur for Victorian Brooklyn. But more recently, Brooklyn's largest park to date, Marine Park, had its dreams. Unfortunately, they became nightmares in the midst of the Great Depression before mostly vanishing into the figments of the Board of Estimate's imagination.

To begin with, what is the Board of Estimate? This was a review board made up of borough presidents that ruled on city expenditures. Eliminated in the latest city charter, its responsibilities are now assumed by the city council.

In 1932, the *New York Herald Tribune* announced that a "seaside resort" capable of "entertaining" 2 million persons had been planned by the parks department for southern Brooklyn. Approved by Parks Commissioner James J. Browne, the plan had been forwarded to the Board of Estimate. At a cost of $30 million (in 1930 dollars), the completed park would occupy 1,848 acres and run three miles along Jamaica Bay, a distance one half mile longer than Central Park.

Within the park would be a 100,000-seat football stadium, a quarter-mile track, three smaller football fields and playing fields, eighty baseball fields plus lacrosse, hurling, cricket and field hockey fields. Twelve archery ranges and forty-eight turf tennis courts were additional. Among the greens would be twelve for lawn bowling, sixty croquet greens, an eighteen-hole golf course and a pitch-and-putt course, as well as sixty-six acres for individual recreation. Additional clay tennis courts (170) would be scattered throughout the park in eight locations. Also planned were ten more concrete courts, which could also be used for outside dancing; three championship courts with a stadium; thirty handball courts; half an acre for quoits, horseshoes and bocce; an indoor hockey rink with stands and a practice rink. And these were just the athletic activities! The list goes on.

The final plan included a casino, but not a gambling casino in the current sense. (In the original Italian, *casino* meant a small lodge used for meetings and entertainment, such as dancing.) The Marine Park casino—to seat one thousand

Proposed bathhouse at Marine Park. *Kingsborough Historical Society*/New York Herald Tribune.

persons—was modeled after the Central Park Casino. Six acres of garden would surround the casino. A "music grove" for symphonic concerts would seat twenty thousand persons, and an outdoor theater would seat ten thousand more. Eight acres of picnic groves; three greenhouses; six acres for a garden nursery; and a two mile, double-decker boardwalk bordering two miles of "ocean-front" beach would also be added. (Did they confuse the bay with the ocean?)

Now comes the "marine" aspect. There were to be three smaller pools for 3,600 bathers each, a bathhouse for 2,800 bathers and spectator stands for 6,000—then another three outdoor pools, an indoor pool and a second bathhouse on Avenue U and the yacht basin. The marina, presumably at Gerritsen Beach, could moor 1,400 yachts with canoe racks for 500 sailing canoes, 2,400 paddling canoes and 2,400 rowboats. A boathouse would hold 411 shells next to a two-mile racing course and a model yacht basin.

The commissioner pointed out that there are 453 acres of water within the park: the Long Canal, the Big Pool, the Outboard Harbor and the Yacht Basin. He alluded to the Olympics and to the Thames course in England, so obviously the goal was to have Brooklyn host a future Olympics. And just as obviously, the dream park was never funded and never happened.

Brooklyn As a World's Fair
October 18, 2007

New York as a city has had its share of World's Fairs, starting with the Crystal Palace in 1853 on Forty-second Street, site of today's New York Public

Library. From 1939–40, the World of Tomorrow showed us the future, and New York's 300th anniversary became the rationale for the 1964–65 fair.

According to international agreements, expositions were originally destined for a six-month life span but later were extended to a year. New York raised the time frame to two years, hence the temporary status of the fairs and their structures. At the Queens site, only the New York City Building remains, having served for two fairs, and from 1965, the rusting New York State performance space, the Unisphere and the Hall of Science.

However, many of the more creative attractions of America's fair ended in Coney Island, giving them an extended life span and allowing publicists to tout Coney as a "permanent" world's fair. This is as close as Brooklyn got to an international exposition.

At Coney Island, Steeplechase Park borrowed the Ferris wheel from Chicago's 1893 Columbia Exposition, while Dreamland used the Creation display from the St. Louis "Louisiana Purchase" Exposition of 1904. Andrew Culver, a railroad mogul, shipped the Sawyer Tower from the 1876 Philadelphia Centennial Exposition and renamed it the Iron Tower.

George Tilyou, a frequent visitor to fairs, convinced Fred Thompson and Elmer Dundy to move their exhibits from the Buffalo Pan-American Exposition (1901) to his Steeplechase. This transfer included their popular "Trip to the Moon" and dual Ferris wheels on a teeter-totter. After Tilyou raised his rent, Thompson and Dundy abandoned Steeplechase and moved their "Moon" exhibit down to their new Luna Park in 1904. Then they imported the Kaleidoscope Tower from St. Louis. Later in the century, Steeplechase brought the Lifesaver Parachute Jump from the 1939 New York World's Fair to the ocean side. In a reverse exchange, Feltman's 1903 Superba carousel traveled from Coney Island to the 1964 New York World's Fair when Astroland replaced the site with its Astrotower.

While these exchanges and other acquisitions are well documented, not many historians are familiar with a proposal for a Brooklyn World's Fair planned for Prospect Park in 1883, as cited in the *Brooklyn Union Argus* on June 2, 1879. The rationale for selecting newly completed Prospect Park as a site centered on its accessible rail transportation. The proposal named the elevation of park grounds for reasons of health, since the recent low-lying Philadelphia fair had been plagued by malaria.

The newspaper wrote that cooler Coney Island was only fifteen minutes from Prospect Park, thereby ensuring "success of the World's Fair in the three hot summer months." The argument reasoned that if visitors "knew that after spending six or eight hours at the fair…they could afterwards, in ten or twelve minutes, be at the ocean side, plunge into the surf and for a few hours gather health, strength, and pleasure amid the gay throngs there," then the Brooklyn World's Fair of 1883 would be an unqualified success.

To cap the argument, the article argued that the financial profit that the cities of Brooklyn and New York might accrue from such an enterprise should clinch the deal. Cool Brooklyn, sylvan Prospect Park and breezy Coney Island would draw the crowds—not hot, unbearable Manhattan.

Needless to say, New York City's next fair was held in 1939, and while it was built over filled-in land called the Brooklyn Ash Works, it occurred in Queens, not Brooklyn.

With Walt Whitman in Fort Greene
January 22, 2009

I met an old gentleman last November. He was wandering around Fort Greene Park—only he called it Fort Washington Park for some reason—handing out snippets of poetry he claimed to have written. Reaching down into a carpetbag valise, he extracted one titled "Crossing Brooklyn Ferry" and handed it to me. I asked, "You mean the yellow water taxi under the Brooklyn Bridge?" "I know of no bridge hereabouts," he replied. "I refer to the *Brooklyn*, the sternwheeler that leaves from the Ferry House by old Fulton Street." Then he shrugged. "These jottings are what I call my 'leaves of grass,'" he said. "My real purpose here is to drum up support for this park to remember the prisoners lost in our War for Independence. You must remember the makeshift tomb over yonder near Irishtown. Well, now we celebrate a memorial fit for the martyrs buried there, those poor souls who died on the warship prisons rotting in Wallabout Bay."

He surveyed the scene—the bunting, the honor guard of soldiers from Washington's army, the fife and drum corps. "Now, at least we have a crypt for their bones as a visible token of their valor, as I wrote in the *Eagle*," he said with a grim smile. "I understand the park is to be renamed after General Nathanael Greene. Good choice!" And he strolled off over a knoll.

Recognition of this good work started in 1844. Championed by Walt Whitman two years later, the tribute reached its apotheosis in 1908 with the dedication of the 148-foot memorial led by Secretary of War and President-Elect William Howard Taft.

Darrel Blaine Ford
portraying Walt Whitman
at Fort Greene. *Photo by
John Manbeck.*

A century later, after decades of neglect, the parks department, the Fort Greene Conservancy and the Society of Old Brooklynites led the agonizing march toward rehabilitating and rededicating the Stanford White–designed Prison Ships Martyrs' Monument on November 15. A history of the infamous years of British occupation is documented in the visitors' center. The daylong public activities added to the ceremonial events. The monument had been cleaned and the urn on top modernized. Four bronze eagles had guarded the base of the monument but were removed from the site in the 1960s to protect them from vandalism and theft. Recast and cleaned, four eagles were unveiled—two originals and two new statues.

Toward the end of the day, the formal commemoration began with speeches, music and a twenty-one-gun salute, culminating in the major event—the relighting of the eternal flame atop the memorial column. The illuminated tribute had been extinguished in 1921.

As the sun settled in the West, I saw the poet sauntering toward his home on Portland Street, his stout walking stick by his side. "I take my hat off to nothing!" cried Walt Whitman, looking back. Then with a deep bow toward the monument, he doffed his soft, broad-brimmed chapeau.

Green Brooklyn: Brooklyn Botanic Garden and Brooklyn Bridge Park
April 22, 2010

With spring (hopefully) in the air, thoughts fly to flowers and green space. Brooklyn is graced with two celebratory green spaces: the Brooklyn Botanic Garden and the new Brooklyn Bridge Park. On top of that, today is Earth Day.

Let's begin with the Botanic Garden. This year, the garden celebrates its centennial year under the directorship of its new president, Scot Medbury—although the garden technically didn't get started until 1911.

The parkland, adjacent to Mount Prospect, a crucial site in the 1776 Battle of Brooklyn in the Revolutionary War, was part of the 1864 Prospect Park land purchase until Flatbush Avenue bisected the parkland. In 1856, Mount Prospect housed a holding tank for the Ridgewood Reservoir owned by the Brooklyn Water Works. By the 1930s, the reservoir became inadequate, and the land was transferred to the parks department as Institute Park, a name derived from the Brooklyn Institute of Arts and Sciences.

The New York State legislature established the Botanic Garden in 1897. Designed by the sons of Frederick Olmsted, the designer of Prospect and Central Parks, the Botanic Garden was managed by the Brooklyn Institute. That organization, part Brooklyn's nineteenth-century "city beautiful" movement, created its cultural arts institutions: the Brooklyn Public Library, the Brooklyn Museum and the Brooklyn Children's Museum. The garden opened to the public on May 13, 1911.

The Native Flora Garden appeared that first year, exhibiting plants native to a one-hundred-mile radius of New York City. This was followed by the Children's Garden in 1914, the Japanese Hill-and-Pond Garden in 1915 and the Rock Garden in 1916. By 1945, Brooklyn's Botanic Garden included over thirteen separate gardens and buildings. Included in later additions were the Shakespeare, Cranford Rose, Osborne, Fragrance, Herb and Discovery Gardens. Among the architectural complements are Magnolia Plaza (1932), Lily Pool Terrace (1921) and the Steinhardt Conservatory (1988). The spring cherry blossom festival in the Cherry Esplanade highlights over two hundred cherry trees and forty-two species.

Palm House, Brooklyn Botanic Garden. *Photo by John Manbeck.*

Another popular site is the Celebrity Path (1985), which winds near the Japanese Garden pond and documents names of famed Brooklynites along the way.

The Botanic Garden also features workshops and outreach programs such as the "Greenest Block in Brooklyn" competition; GreenBridge, a community horticulture program to foster local garden programs; and the Urban Composting Project.

A celebration for the centennial will include a birthday party on June 12 and lectures on bee keeping but will undoubtedly start with the April and May flowering of the cherry trees. Other activities will occur in July, August and September. This year also marks the groundbreaking for a new visitors' center, a "green" building with a living roof, scheduled to open next year.

Nearby Brooklyn Bridge Park, on the other hand, is the newest of the borough's parks, and a section of it opened officially on March 22. On that rainy Monday, hilly, winding paths created on the former site of Pier 1 offered an attractive vista of the Manhattan skyline from a vantage point jutting into the East River. The following day, First Lady Michelle Obama

Brooklyn Bridge Park. *Photo by John Manbeck.*

and her children made an unannounced visit to the park while en route to film scenes for *Sesame Street.*

Wandering through this small eight-acre portion of the future eighty-five-acre park (to be the city's largest), one can observe how our other parks—Prospect, Botanic Garden, Central—were created by man. Still working on building and shaping the park, the Skanska Company has built a beautiful oasis on Brooklyn's waterfront. With the eventual demolition of the mammoth National Cold Storage Company warehouse, the Brooklyn skyline will open up to even more splendors such as a kayak channel.

Next to open this spring will be Pier 6 at Atlantic Avenue. The first phase of the park construction is expected to be completed by 2013. Questions of finance, development and control are yet to be answered, and these problems challenged projects in the past, including the construction of the Brooklyn Bridge. Halfway into the bridge's construction, the bridge corporation was sued because experts predicted it would interfere with nautical transportation. The plaintiff wanted the half-completed bridge torn down. He lost.

Perhaps when we begin to enjoy the completed park, all those unpleasant objections will become passé.

Brooklyn Promenade, Not an Esplanade
December 22, 2011

The creation of the Promenade that abuts Brooklyn Heights is as unique as the Brooklyn Bridge to its north—both are iconic. Henrik Krogius, an editor at the *Brooklyn Eagle*, has written a valuable new text about the unusual history that brought the Promenade into fruition titled *The Brooklyn Heights Promenade* (The History Press). As editor of the *Brooklyn Heights Press and Cobble Hill News*, Krogius presents insider information and tenacious reportage to ferret out the origins of the controversial project. His background as an architectural student facilitated the engineering aspects involved. Included are rare photographs of construction by amateur photographer Louise Casey, who lived on Columbia Heights and documented the activity.

Krogius points out that the scope of the project affected residents of Columbia Heights the most because their back gardens were sacrificed. Others did not know or care because World War II occupied their concerns. The waterfront below the Heights was a world described by Ernest Poole in his 1915 novel *The Harbor*—a dangerous world of sailors and longshoremen and piers and warehouses.

Part 1 of Krogius's book deals with the back story of the Promenade and how it evolved from Robert Moses's argument for a circumferential highway to speed military transportation among the many forts and installations around the perimeter of Brooklyn and Queens. The Belt Parkway and Brooklyn-Queens Expressway were integral sections of this network. The roadway was planned for speed, cutting through the center of Sheepshead Bay, Red Hook, along Hicks Street in Brooklyn Heights and splitting Williamsburg.

But it never happened in Brooklyn Heights, and this is the story of the Promenade. Krogius details how this occurred, who was (possibly) responsible and what the long-range effects were. He has researched public records, Brooklyn Heights Association records, the *Eagle* library, Long Island Historical Society files and Brooklyn College's archives. He has also interviewed surviving participants and has duplicated personal correspondence between Commissioner Moses and himself when he was a U.S. Air Force lieutenant.

Snow on the Promenade. *Photo by John Manbeck.*

Photographs from Louise Casey, official files and Krogius's personal collection are supplemented by drawings of plans and local scenes. The Promenade, he concludes, was a "lucky afterthought" and is unique in the world.

Among the little-known facts that Krogius reveals is the preservation role played by Gladys Underwood James (of typewriter fame), who bought up Columbia Heights brownstones to save them. While Hicks and Columbia Heights were basically preserved, the cantilevered roadways that hung on the Brooklyn palisade took out Washington Roebling's house, from which he watched construction of the Brooklyn Bridge, as well as the "Writers' House" or "February House" on Middagh Street. (A musical about the writers who lived there in the 1940s will open this February at the Public Theater.)

The author also reveals that the empty pedestal base on the Promenade at Orange Street was built for a sculpture in tribute to the Roeblings— Washington, Emily and John—but the Brooklyn Heights Association never funded it.

The year 1945 is marked as the date for the creation of the roadways that eventually led to the Promenade. By 1946, the Montague Street cut, which

Montague Terrace sitting park, circa 1947. *Brooklyn Public Library, Brooklyn Collection.*

accessed the docks and the Wall Street ferry by trolley, was filled in, and the Montague Terrace viewing platform (a predecessor of the Promenade) was demolished. In a lovely paean, Krogius gives tribute to the Penny Bridge that crossed Montague Street but did not survive construction.

Part 2 of the book consists of reprints of the author's articles on the construction, including the threat posed by the Port of New York Authority to allow structures of up to seventy feet, blocking views from the Promenade as well as from the houses. This issue was settled with the special zoning—Special Scenic District. The removal of the piers for Brooklyn Bridge Park sealed the controversy.

Henry Stern, then New York City parks commissioner, officially named the one-third-mile walk the Brooklyn Heights Promenade. Pictures in the book support the magnetic attraction of the Promenade and show strollers, joggers, dancers, dog walkers, acrobats and tourists, tourists, tourists. Movie companies and commercial photographers flock there (remember the scene from *The French Connection?*) Krogius calls it "a magnificent creation of inadvertence" and notes that "the babble of tongues heard on the Promenade even includes English."

Both the Promenade and the book are successes. Take a walk on Brooklyn's wild side—buy the book for someone you love.

Jane's Carousel Comes to Brooklyn
September 29, 2011

With the recent opening of Jane's Carousel in Dumbo, a great Brooklyn tradition has been revived. Carousels have long been a significant part of Brooklyn's history. Many of these wonderful rides were created and flourished in Coney Island, at the other end of the borough.

One of the oldest and most cherished amusements, the popularity of the carousels emerged from the age of the equestrian and can be traced back to the Byzantines. Adapted from the Italian word *carousello*, the ride has been powered by humans, donkeys, ponies, steam and, eventually, electric machinery. The horses and other beasts riding the carousel—including a hippocampus, a mythical half horse/half dolphin—were hand carved by craftsmen who prided themselves on creating stately artworks.

In Victorian Coney Island, carousels were commissioned by restaurants, bathhouses and other amusements to lure in the passersby. Several schools of carvers prided themselves on unique designs so that horses carved in Philadelphia or Denver or Germany stood apart from the wild steeds that came out of Coney's factories. One of the earliest and foremost carvers was Danish artisan Charles Looff, who worked from 1875 in his Gravesend factory until he moved to Long Beach, California, in 1905. In 1903, Charles Feltman commissioned Marcus Illions to build a carousel for the entrance to his restaurants. In his Coney Island factory, William Mangels created the mechanism to make horses rise and fall. Along with Illions, other superb carvers, such as Charles Carmel, Solomon Stein and Harry Goldstein, created memorable horses and rides.

The most elaborate carousel was the El Dorado, built in 1910 in Leipzig, Germany, by Hugo Hasse, who then shipped it to Dreamland's amusement park. Standing forty-two feet high, it featured three platforms in tiers operating at different speeds. Illuminated by six thousand lights, it was housed in an octagonal building. When Dreamland burned in 1911, the carousel was rescued by George Tilyou for his Steeplechase, where it remained until 1966. Steeplechase also had the Chanticleer, a merry-go-round of all chickens that stood on Surf Avenue outside the Pavilion of Fun.

Jane's Carousel in Brooklyn Bridge Park. *Photo by John Manbeck.*

The B&B Carousell, also owned by the Tilyou family, operated on Surf Avenue. Built in 1932, it will surface again on the Boardwalk outside the baseball stadium. Luna Park, the original one, owned two carousels built in 1909 and 1924. The one at Brighton Beach Baths was built in 1879.

Original rides were more elaborate, with jewel-studded bridles, buckles and belts decorating elegant horses. Twenty-five carousels operated in Coney Island alone. As the Coney Island style developed, the horses became wilder and fiercer, with flowing manes, clenched teeth and glaring eyes. A 1914 Coney Island carousel with fifty-one horses ended up in Prospect Park, and another, built in 1917, ended up in Disney World.

Rival companies followed the Coney Island craftsmen into the business. A prime competitor was the Philadelphia Toboggan Company, founded in Hatfield, Pennsylvania, in 1904. This is the oldest surviving roller coaster company, and it manufactured Jane's Carousel. The company built carousels, roller coasters and skee-ball games. Between 1904 and 1930, it constructed seventy-five carousels, thirty-six of which remain.

Jane's Carousel is located in Brooklyn Bridge Park, with a background of the Tobacco Warehouse and Empire Stores, and is moored under the Brooklyn Bridge in a square acrylic building. Built in 1922, Ms. Jane Walentas acquired it and its forty-eight horses from a Youngstown, Ohio amusement park. Within its distinctive Jean Nouvel–designed illuminated home, it stands as Brooklyn's latest welcome monument to the carousel tradition.

Part V

FOOD AND DRINK

Beer Garden Revival
August 11, 2011

For many years, Brooklyn reigned as the beer capital of New York. In the 1880s, Williamsburg and Greenpoint harbored over eighty local brewers, mostly of German origin. Famous names such as Rheingold, Trommer's, Ulmer and Conrad Eurich breweries dominated those upstarts from Milwaukee. In the rear of breweries, gardens with umbrella-ed tables offered respite from hot summer days. The German community in Coney Island—fostered by Feltman's and Bauer's—served local beer, overflowing with Coney Island heads.

It all started back when immigrant Germans occupied the Lower East Side, calling it *Kleinedeutschland*, or Little Germany. Today, it would be in East Village and Chinatown. On Second Avenue, the New York Public Library building has the word *Bibliothek* carved above the entrance, which is next to the former German Dispensary. In 1824, Castle Garden in Battery Park was New York's first beer garden before it materialized as the official immigration processing station, eventually superseded by Ellis Island.

Then, in 1919, Prohibition came crashing down, driving out many of these local Brooklyn brewers. The survivors stabilized in the '30s, but the baseball strike of the '40s laid waste to all but the strongest. Milwaukee and St. Louis moved in for the kill, taking over companies and moving them to

Radegast Hall & Beer Garden in Williamsburg. *Photo by John Manbeck.*

Manhattan and, even worse, out of the city. Several decades ago, a German restaurant was difficult to find outside of Rolf's on the East Side and Franklin Square on Long Island, much less a beer garden. Even in Yorktown, a former German stronghold, they had been gentrified out of existence.

In 1987, Steve Hindy came to the rescue when he founded Brooklyn Beer in Williamsburg, with other local craft brewers following close behind him. Now the old beer garden has returned and is thriving in the hipster neighborhoods and even further out there. What's more, the *New York Times* has noted its arrival with the observation that Williamsburg could be mistaken for Bavaria in Oktoberfest.

With over fifty-four *biergartens* in the city and an app for your mobile phone (Beer Gardens NYC), the time of the beer garden has obviously arrived. Many gardens follow the customs of Munich, such as the Radegast Hall & Beer Garden on North Third Street in Williamsburg, home to communal tables serving all sizes and shapes of sausages, including bratwurst, and schnitzel. Other beer gardens—real or pseudo—in Billyburg can be found on weekends at the Brooklyn Brewery on North Eleventh Street, on Berry

Street at Berry Park, at the Loreley on Frost Street and at Spuyten Duyvil on Metropolitan Avenue.

But the joy has spread to Greenpoint, where Spritzenhaus can be found on Nassau Avenue by McCarren Park. Some of these watering holes used to be pubs but have switched to capture the spirit of the moment. Prospect Heights has a couple: Franklin Park at St. John's Place and Washington Commons on Washington Avenue. Across Flatbush Avenue in Park Slope, you can find the Fourth Avenue Pub and Mission Dolores, also on Fourth. Carroll Gardens has the old standby on Smith Street, the Gowanus Yacht Club. Out on Stillwell Avenue in Coney Island, you can find Beer Island. While Brooklyn Heights hasn't named an official beer garden yet, residents and visitors can find them on Front Street in Dumbo: Café-Bar, Brooklyn Bridge Gardens and Gastro Pub. While over in Fort Green, there's Der Schwarze Kölner on Fulton Street, which means almost what you think it means.

As you can deduce, beer gardens have sprung up in other parts of the city, but in this column, only Brooklyn history need be cited.

Ice Cream for Brooklyn
July 7, 2005

The dog days of summer scream for refreshment. More ice cream is consumed in July than in any other month. July, in fact, is National Ice Cream Month!

In the past, we rushed for the cool Flatbush ice cream parlors: Karp's, Henry's, Jentz's and Jahn's. (Remember the Kitchen Sink?) Others searched for a Howard Johnson's (can you name all twenty-six flavors?), Peter's or even a genteel Schrafft's. For stay-at-homes, the Good Humor truck, with its summer jingle bells, brought curbside service. (Ever win a free ice cream with a "lucky stick?")

Now you drive or walk to storefronts for the pricey Baskin-Robbins, Häagen-Dazs (named because it *sounded* Danish), Ben & Jerry's, maybe a Hershey's or the still-popular Carvel. Other shops include Once Upon a Sundae ice cream parlor in Bay Ridge, Tom's Restaurant on Washington Avenue in Prospect Heights, Brooklyn Farmacy in Carroll Gardens, Uncle Luigi's at Prospect Park, a chain called Taste of the Tropics in Flatbush and the Brooklyn Ice Cream Factory at Fulton Ferry. But mostly it's eat, drip and run.

Original Häagen-Dazs shop on Montague Street, Brooklyn Heights. *Photo by John Manbeck.*

Egg cream—a cheaper refreshment—is strictly Brooklyn. Created by Brooklynite Louis Auster in 1890, the drink may have originally contained both eggs and cream. But it definitely featured half-ounces of Fox's U-Bet chocolate syrup from another Brooklyn firm that's still in business. A dash of milk and squirts of Brooklyn seltzer were added, but no ice cream—that would make the drink too expensive.

Ice cream originally graced the tables of the European rich and royal. In Europe, ice cream was a familiar luxury since the Roman times. Snow and ice were imported from the mountains to cool the emperor's fruit drinks. Apocryphally, Marco Polo brought ice cream (as well as spaghetti) from Asia to Rome. In Italy, the descendant is the superb *gelato*, with flavors not duplicated in America.

The Italian owner of Café Procope in Paris offered ice cream on his menu in 1660, while another Italian, Tortoni, sold *biscuit tortoni* to Parisians. Today, in Paris, the *crème de la crème* is Bertillon ice cream, from a family business that routinely closes for the summer months of July and August. Now the brand is franchised to exclusive restaurants.

Here in America, Philip Lenzi, a London caterer, opened an "iced cream shoppe" in New York in 1774. An African American confectioner from Philadelphia, Augustus Jackson sold several ice cream recipes in 1832. Nancy Johnson from New Jersey invented the hand-cranked freezer in 1846, which froze an ice cream mix in a bed of salt and ice. By 1851, Jacob Fussel started the first ice cream factory in Baltimore.

Among our royalty, George Washington owned two pewter "ice cream pots," Mrs. Alexander Hamilton served ice cream regularly and the famous Dolley

Madison, wife of President James Madison, served her favorite—mounds of strawberry ice cream—at her husband's 1813 inaugural ball. Supposedly, she had procured the recipe from a freed African American in Delaware, Aunt Sallie Shadd, who used a combination of frozen cream, sugar and fruit. Over in Philadelphia, William Breyer created his famous brand in 1866.

The "hokey pokey" predecessor to the ice cream cone consisted of mixed flavors and colors made from cornstarch and milk. It was served in a paper cup and cost one penny. The word came from the Italian *occipocci*. Popularized at the Philadelphia Centennial's Fair in 1876, it materialized as an ice cream soda in 1879, created by Fred Sanders of Detroit.

By the time the Louisiana Purchase Exposition opened in St. Louis in 1904, the ice cream cone appeared. Many inventors claim credit for this creation. Italo Marchiony, who had operated a pushcart in New York since 1896, was issued a patent for a cone in 1903. Then there is Charles Menches from Hamburg, New York, who also claimed creation of the hamburger, or Ernest Hamwi, a Syrian waffle salesman who insisted his *zalabia* was the first cone. And Abe Doumar, David Avayou and Arnold Fornachou. All were among the fifty ice cream stands at the St. Louis Fair.

The concept was not lost on Frederic Thompson, architect of Coney Island's Luna Park, who intentionally designed the amusement park's second tower in the shape of an upside-down ice cream cone.

Soda fountains, popularly known as "sanitary soda fountains" in several Coney Island locations, had been patented in 1819. One hundred years later, Archie Kohr invented a frozen custard machine in York, Pennsylvania, and moved it to Coney Island's boardwalk, where he sold 18,460 cones at five cents each the first weekend.

By 1921, the Eskimo Pie—a chocolate-covered ice cream bar—was created by Chris Nelson near Brooklyn, Iowa. Henry Burt of Youngstown, Ohio, expanded the concept in 1923 with his Good Humor on a stick, while Epperson of California gave us the Popsicle in 1926 and Samuel Isaly of Pittsburgh added the Klondike Bar in 1929. The ice cream "sundae," invented in Evanston, Illinois, was only sold on Sundays, but the spelling was changed to avoid charges of blasphemy. Tom Carvel created his mix of soft ice cream in 1939. In 1989, Custard's Last Stand opened in Kansas.

Back in Brooklyn, we had Bassett's, sold in Coney Island and manufactured by the Paris Ice Cream Company. The Gold Seal Riviera Ice Cream Company started here in 1932, followed by Alpen-Zauber Ice Cream. In the 1930s, over ninety-nine ice cream factories operated in New York City. By the 1940s, an "ice cream for breakfast" movement started.

Remember what the "Kitchen Sink" contained? Small stuff compared to the *biggest ever* ice cream sundae created in Anaheim, California, in 1985. It stood twelve feet high, contained 4,667 gallons of ice cream and 7,000 pounds of toppings.

Today, the ice cream industry is an $11 billion retail industry. In spite of Ben & Jerry, the three most popular flavors are vanilla, chocolate and butter pecan. The United States is the top ice cream–consuming country, followed by New Zealand and Denmark.

And now let's follow the bouncing ball and sing the last verse of "The Ice Cream Song," written by Johnson, Moll & King and popularized by Fred Waring and his Pennsylvanians:

> *Just to show how tough they were*
> *All those Eskimos began to holler:*
> *"Iceberg, Lindbergh, Sol Berg and Ginzberg*
> *Ice Cream Cohen.*
> *I scream, you scream, everybody wants ice cream.*
> *Rah, rah, raaazberry!"*

Green Market Day
May 12, 2005

Fred Wilklow drives his truck from upstate Highland, New York, to Borough Hall every Tuesday, Thursday and Saturday. Since 1985, he and members from his family have offered freshly picked fruit (and warm cider in winter) to Brooklynites at Brooklyn's Green Market.

At least ten other stands join him in selling fresh produce, flowers, baked goods and, occasionally, fish. Recently, the market moved from the steps of Borough Hall to Columbus Park in front of the Supreme Court building because the market trucks were breaking the bluestone sidewalks.

The Green Markets that now seem ubiquitous around the city have a history going back to the Dutch settlers. In New Amsterdam, Market Street thronged with so many purveyors that Friday was declared a weekly "market day" in 1641 to regulate trade. Unofficially, we continue to recognize the day with food ads that flood the newspapers on Thursdays. By 1656, the first public market was built to protect the merchants against "hucksters" or unregulated peddlers.

Under both British and later American rule, the New York City Common Council supervised all markets, including slave markets. In 1816, the Fulton Fish Market opened its stalls. The most important figure in nineteenth-century markets was the butcher, with his top hat and apron tied over a long-tailed coat. An infamous Brooklyn butcher was William Poole, a gang leader who protested Irish immigration in the Nativist riots and was later dramatized in *The Gangs of New York*. Bill "The Butcher" Poole was buried in Green-Wood Cemetery in 1855.

An age of perishable food and poverty drove many immigrant women and children to become itinerant peddlers of fruits, vegetables, candies and pies. By 1866, pushcarts made life simpler. New York peddlers flocked to Hester Street in Manhattan's Lower East Side, whereas Wallabout Market served as Brooklyn's market center. Here the marketers gathered by Wallabout Bay, which had been settled by Walloons (Flemish) in 1637. The land there had been purchased by one of Brooklyn's first settlers, Joris Jansen de Rapalje. That same vicinity infamously became associated with the British prison ships that were moored there during the American Revolution. The City of Brooklyn reserved a section between Flushing and Clinton Streets from the Brooklyn Navy Yard for the Wallabout Market in 1890. The commercial location remained there until World War II, when the federal government reclaimed it for an expanded Navy Yard.

In attempts to regulate trade, sanitation and health in the market, a Pushcart Commission was established in 1905. In 1917, it evolved into the Department of Markets. The administration of Mayor Fiorello LaGuardia abolished all open pushcart markets in the 1930s. With the arrival of supermarkets and improvement in refrigeration, crops no longer needed to be grown locally. But the public still wanted freshly grown fruits and vegetables rather than frozen or hothouse-raised produce. Pressured by rural farmers who saw their businesses being taken over by conglomerates, New York City introduced the first Green Market farmers' market in 1976. Today, sixteen markets have spread throughout Manhattan Island. The original at Union Square attracts over twenty thousand customers. The Greenmarket Program is supervised by the Council on the Environment of New York City.

Green markets, some open year-round, can be found in every borough. Brooklyn's Wallabout Market was replaced by the Brooklyn Terminal Market in Flatlands with over twenty-four vendors who sell retail and wholesale. Of Brooklyn's greenmarkets, the Borough Hall and Prospect Park markets are the oldest and most popular.

Split schedules allow farmers to grow and harvest their crops and sell them without a middleman. Most open at 8:00 a.m. Brooklyn markets can

Brooklyn Farmers' Market. *Photo by John Manbeck.*

be found in the following locations: Borough Hall, Albee Square, Grand Army Plaza, Windsor Terrace, Bedford-Stuyvesant, Williamsburg and McCarren Park.

Urban Farming Returns to Its Roots
May 23, 2012

Professor Babette Audant pulled a carrot from the earth, brushed off the loose dirt and took a bite. Her students looked on, mildly horrified. "But it's dirty," one exclaimed. "It's cleaner and healthier than most of the foods you eat," she responded.

Audant, petite, lively and dedicated, supervises the urban farm program at Kingsborough Community College (KCC) on the former sands of Manhattan Beach. With the assistance of a staff of dedicated gardeners including Andrew Cooper, an employee of Active Citizens Project, the college's partner; Mara Gittleman, assistant farm manager and KCC instructor; and a crew of volunteers who don't mind getting their fingers dirty, Audant has succeeded in coaxing seedlings and sprouts out of the ground this first spring. Much of the cold-weather nurturing occurs in a plastic-covered hothouse set up next to the seedbeds. Eventually, the produce will be served in the school's kitchens and in local farmers' markets.

Brooklyn's association with the soil has a long history. Until post–World War II, farms scattered throughout southern Brooklyn raised vegetables, fruit and even marketed milk from local cows and goats. In 2000, *Brooklyn, Of Cabbages and Kings County: Agriculture and the Formation of Modern Brooklyn* by Marc Linder and Lawrence Zacharis, neither of whom came from Brooklyn, revealed the scope of agriculture in Brooklyn's past. They concluded that Brooklyn's ties to the earth helped shape its future.

Kingsborough's farm started in March 2011 with raised beds of transplanted seedlings. The urban garden, in a remote area of the campus between two temporary buildings, broke ground in March with fifteen beds and a goal of twenty-seven beds to be filled with greens. Audant, executive director of the KCC Center for Economic and Workforce Development, broke off a leaf and offered it to me. "It's chocolate mint," she explained. And it did have a taste of chocolate.

As an extension of the culinary program in the college's Tourism and Hospitality Department, the program has an important educational goal. Food is central to the spaces we inhabit, Audant believes. Her field of study is geography, and she feels that hot sauce is the food basic to many of Brooklyn's cultures. Chili peppers will be a prime food item in their urban garden. Future plans call for an expanded herb garden (because of the smells and the colors) and a therapeutic garden for plants used in hospitals and nursing homes. "The very act of gardening can be therapeutic," Audant said. She hopes to incorporate beekeeping to understand pollination. In their classes, students learn about the benefits and dangers of food. Some classes are paired with academic subjects to broaden the horizons of the students.

The Kingsborough program is the most recent of courses with an agricultural focus that are seeping into the academic curriculum of Brooklyn's colleges and public schools. While KCC expands horticulture on the southern shore, City Tech is stimulating a similar interest downtown Brooklyn.

The New York City College of Technology doesn't have the luxury of garden space on its downtown campus, so its Hospitality Garden grows in the DeKalb Market. As at Kingsborough, students learn that vegetables do not grow in cans or in the freezer. When they harvest them, they discover the

Professor Babette Audant at the Kingsborough Community College Urban Farm. *Photo by John Manbeck.*

exciting difference between fresh and processed produce, according to City Tech professor Patrick O'Halloran.

Brooklyn's secondary schools are returning to the soil as well. Farm projects have surfaced in Bushwick and East Flatbush, where Farm School NYC and the Urban Farm School have started. The rationale behind these new incentives is to reintroduce city pupils to their foods and educate them on how nutrition is a vital component of their lives.

Earlier generations of Brooklyn pupils worked in "victory gardens" during World War II, when gardening appealed to patriotic pride. Schools often boasted of a strip of green growing in the back of the schoolyard. In those days, agriculture was a familiar commodity, with Brooklyn's Wallabout and Washington city markets within easy reach of transportation.

But with the new focus on our agrarian roots taught at Kingsborough, farms have returned to Brooklyn with an educational element. Tomorrow's students will be better informed about what and how to eat, and be healthier for it.

Part VI

BREUCKELEN: OLD AND NEW

Dutch Treat
September 17, 2009

As you may have heard, Brooklyn has been in Dutch for many years, say four hundred, and this year joins with the city of Santa Fe, New Mexico, in celebrating its birthday. With our abundance of Dutch farmhouses—from Wyckoffs to Lotts to Lefferts—we still live with our Dutch ancestors. Relics of our Dutch origins can be discovered in all five boroughs, as well as in architecture and vestiges of language: boss from *baas*, cookies from *koeckjes*, Brooklyn "stoops" and Santa Claus from *Sinterklaas*. Festivities abound these weeks, with celebrations on Governors' Island (or Nutten Island), the first Dutch settlement; South Street Seaport; the Museum of the City of New York; and Brooklyn's historic Wyckoff Homestead.

As Russell Shorto has pointed out in his sharp analysis of the Dutch experience in *The Island at the Center of the World*, our American heritage owes more to the Dutch than to the English. Whereas the seventeenth-century Dutch were traders and intellectuals, the English who arrived in New England were more autocratic and theocratic, stemming from their associations with Oliver Cromwell, the dictatorial leader of England.

In the seventeenth century, the Netherlands stood at the center of European culture and intellectual curiosity. Having wrested off the shackles of Spanish control, the Dutch embarked on a mission to explore the world for commercial ends. Only the English had established a competitive challenge.

In 1607, the Dutch fleet defeated the Spanish armada at Gibraltar, and in 1609, the Dutch East India Company contracted with Henry Hudson to discover new trading routes. Hudson's contact at Coney Island and the subsequent murder of his mate, John Coleman, spurred a recent query by *New York Times* writer Sam Roberts into solving this early crime.

By 1621, the newly formed Dutch West India Company had been granted a monopoly to settle the trading post of New Netherland, which reached fruition in 1624. When the third governor-general, Peter Minuit, arrived in 1626, "bought" Manhattan Island and built Fort Amsterdam, the post began to resemble a colony rather than a business enterprise. Around this time, the newcomers turned their attention south across the East River and made several land "purchases" from the native Lenapes, who probably did not understand the concept, according to historian Kenneth Jackson. Between 1636 and 1684, after the British occupied the Dutch property, Brooklyn lands were transferred to Europeans in over two dozen deeds. Among the Dutch purchases were tracts in Flatlands (New Amersfoort), by Wallabout Bay, and in Gowanus. In 1642, a ferry service was established between Brooklyn and New Amsterdam, a step that increased interaction between the two areas. Kieft's War, between the Dutch and natives, also started that year. Willem Kieft, the governor, invited several English groups to settle in outlying areas as a safety buffer for New Amsterdam on Manhattan. The Brooklyn colony was led by Lady Deborah Moody, who inhabited Gravesend at Kieft's invitation.

Kieft's successor, Peter Stuyvesant, became the most influential and colorful of the administrators. Under his rule, which began in 1647, the Town of Midwout (Flatbush) was founded, the Peter Claeson Wyckoff Homestead was constructed, the Flatbush Dutch Reformed Church was organized and the Town of Gravesend "purchased" Conye Islant. Other towns, such as New Utrecht and Boswijck (Bushwick), materialized before the British captured New Amsterdam in 1664, although the Dutch recaptured the colony in 1673 and renamed it New Orange until the Treaty of Westminster in 1674.

In the first census held in 1790, eighty thousand Dutch immigrants and their descendants were counted among New York's residents. The original Dutch records had an arduous journey from New Amsterdam to London to Albany, where they survived a fire in the New York State Library. Shorto's book evolved from the studious translations of Charles Gehring, the director of the New Netherland Project, who laboriously translated the colloquial Dutch to modern English for American history.

Other original documents from the National Archives of the Netherlands are included at South Street Seaport in this 400th birthday party for New York.

Old Fulton Street Is New Again
October 14 and 21, 2010

The evolution of downtown's Fulton Street started shortly after Robert Fulton docked the *Nassau* on Brooklyn's shores. Today, after a half-century downturn, its growth is assured to continue. On one end, Brooklyn Bridge Park is blossoming; across the street, Dumbo welcomes a plethora of new activity; and at the southern end, in the heart of Downtown Brooklyn, the former Fulton Mall is being repaved, reconfigured and reopened.

Fulton Street—today's *Old* Fulton Street—started inconspicuously enough as Ferry Road, although the British rechristened it "Kings Highway" during their visit here. Once Fulton berthed at Brooklyn, things really began to happen. The *WPA Guide* describes the initial neighborhood as a "waterfront hamlet" that grew into "Brooklyn's Bowery" by 1936 as a result of the commercial base of businesses, warehouses and ferry traffic that developed at the water's edge.

Not only did poet Walt Whitman live at 170 Fulton Street (near Cranberry at that time), but earlier, pamphleteer Tom Paine lived on the corner of Fulton and Sands Streets while French statesman Charles Talleyrand-Perigord lived in a farmhouse on Fulton and Hicks Streets. Those addresses should give you a clue that the course of Fulton's path has changed. Otherwise, how in the world was Fulton Street, which today ceases at Borough Hall, connected to the ferry? Simply because Fulton Street was "de-named" after the elevated train tracks that shrouded it were torn down and the state courthouse facing Columbus Park was constructed. Cadman Plaza West assumed the Fulton name, while Washington Street, on the other side of the park, became Cadman Plaza East.

Cadman Plaza West originally touched the East River until history buffs and preservationists persuaded the city in the 1980s to rename the section Old Fulton Street from the Fulton Ferry Landing (which could have been called George Washington's Jumping-Off Place) to Henry Street. The southern section, where the elevated BMT train cut next to Borough Hall, has been converted into a nameless pedestrian mall.

The main portion of Fulton Street, once called Main Street, had been an Indian path to Jamaica Pass and the section near the river, Clover Hill, an area of rich farms. Today, it is the major thoroughfare through Bedford-Stuyvesant to Jamaica Avenue and Broadway, where it finally skips and sputters to an end. Because of Brooklyn Bridge Park and the growth of

Dumbo, the future of Old Fulton Street seems bright. In April, reports from the *Brooklyn Daily Eagle* announced the possibility of a new building with a restaurant that would reinvigorate the area. Today, Fulton Street is guarded by landmarked history: the Brooklyn Bridge, the Eagle Warehouse and the Brooklyn City Railroad Company Building.

Reports from the 1886 pages of the *Brooklyn Daily Eagle* cite Fulton Street as the commercial strip leading to the ferry comparable to Manhattan's busy Broadway. Fashionable Hicks Street in Brooklyn Heights served as Brooklyn's Fifth Avenue. By 1892, the old *Brooklyn Eagle* had outgrown its offices and printing plant, moving to Johnson Street, with the old printing press section becoming the core for a new warehouse.

On Upper Fulton Street in 1893, gentility was still reflected in the orchards, the mansions (the Lefferts Estate was there), a hunting lodge, cows at Clinton Avenue, tannery shops and stables and the Capitoline Ball Grounds and Skating Pond (1863–80). A year later, the *Eagle* noted that "old Brooklyn is fast fading away," although farms and gardens could still be found in Brooklyn Heights. The "Beecher Boats"—Sunday ferries that brought followers of Henry Ward Beecher from Manhattan to Brooklyn— still shepherded crowds to hear the "Shakespeare of the pulpit."

On Fulton and Pierrepont Streets, Dominick Colgan served delicious meals at his Little Oyster Parlor. Montague and Hicks Streets were considered "uptown." Farther east on Fulton Street and Clinton Avenue stood Walter Lockwood's Dry Goods Emporium (department store), whose aisles were so wide that "a team of horses could be driven down [them]." The ferry landing area, busy with stores in 1896 in spite of the new bridge overhead, was being referred to as Lower Fulton Street. Among the businesses were a tobacco warehouse, a saddle maker, a wholesale grocery, a sail maker and a bank, the Long Island Safe Deposit Company.

A question emerged about the duplication of street names once the consolidation was completed. Should there be two Fulton Streets? Two years later, though, the character of the ferry district was changing, with police in disguises (they shaved off their mustaches) "driving women of questionable character from Fulton Street." The waterfront became further industrialized in 1900, when the New York Dock Company consolidated the waterfront between Fulton Street and the Erie Basin into forty piers with 150 stores and warehouses. By 1901, crime had spread from the waterfront to Upper Fulton Street when youths with a "dice box" robbed a milkman.

In 1924, the ferry ceased operation, and the large ferry terminal built in 1865 was demolished after a fire. The hamlet that the *WPA Guide* referred to

Intersection of Fulton and Jay Streets in the 1950s. *Brooklyn Public Library, Brooklyn Collection.*

was transformed into a "slum." The text refers to the section as a "Brooklyn Bowery, with flophouses, small shops, rancid restaurants, haunted by vagabonds and derelicts." To help restore Fulton Street, the Kings County Elevated Railway, which had started in 1888 and ran to Nostrand Avenue, ceased operation in 1940, followed by demolition of the structure. Tracks and yards formerly used by the railway became S. Cadman Parkes Plaza. In 1937, the city built a warehouse under the bridge.

Changes became more obvious in 1977, when the Landmarks Commission designated the area the Fulton Ferry Historic District. In 1983, the Port Authority stopped cargo ship operation on Piers 1–6. Pete's Downtown, Grimaldi's Pizza, the River Café and Bargemusic arrived, demonstrating that they could turn things around. The landing was rebuilt, and New York Water Taxis made ferry stops. The Purchase Building, a landmark, was demolished by the parks department for parkland.

With the opening of Pier 1 at Brooklyn Bridge Park this year, Brooklynites can see the potential for Lower Fulton Street. With greater interest and activities, it could soon become the apex of the new transportation hub of the Brooklyn waterfront. Upper Fulton Street, long on history, with its iconic historic buildings underneath the cheap façades, deserves a fresh face. It could and should be a tourist destination. (The Downtown Walking Tour podcast guides tourists around these sites.)

Changes have come rapidly to Fulton Street. In 2005, it was co-named Harriet Ross Tubman Avenue, after the abolitionist. The commercial attraction for the street is being revitalized from the days when big department stores along the street made it the shopping Mecca of Brooklyn. H&M, the Swedish superstore, is moving into the former Albee Mall, with talk of Target, J.C. Penney, Kohl's and Nordstrom joining it and Macy's, formerly Abraham & Straus. The latest suggestion has been an Apple store for the street level of the Municipal Building across from Borough Hall on Joralemon Street, the continuation of Fulton Street. With new hotels joining the Fulton Street neighborhood, some of its past glory may be realized.

While it is refreshing to see changes in the Fulton Mall section between Flatbush and Adams Streets, it would have been more desirable to have a real pedestrian mall, with only electric buses running the length of the strip. Continuation of the city routes destroys the image of safe pedestrian access.

Long live Fulton Street!

Gowanus: No More Lavender
October 16, 2008

Once, Gowanus filled a major slice of Brooklyn real estate. Named South Brooklyn because it occupied geography south of the original town of Brooklyn in Brooklyn Heights, it eventually fragmented into the less fragrant neighborhoods of Carroll Gardens, Cobble Hill, Park Slope, Columbia Waterfront District and Red Hook. While some of these other sections have more prosaic names, Gowanus thrived on the industry brought to its shores, its characters and the infamous canal.

Settled by the Dutch in 1636 and probably named after a sachem of the Canarsee Indians, Gowane, the sylvan shores of Gowanus Bay bore scant resemblance to today's industrialized community. The lone business was a distillery owned by the Pierrepont family. Oysters and clams—big ones—were plentiful. Many frame houses date back to the pre-industrial days of gristmills. Long used as a port, the inlet of Gowanus Creek was extended into a canal in the 1840s to manage tidal marshes. Then, in 1868, the Litchfield property

Gowanus Canal bridge in the 1940s. *Brooklyn Public Library, Brooklyn Collection.*

was dredged to offer access to warehouses and heavy industry. As industry dominated the area after the 1860s, the population expanded, particularly transient seamen and workers. But pollution also followed.

Popularly known as the Gashouse District because of the utility tanks, the canal was lined with coal yards, lumberyards, paint and ink manufacturers and paper mills. This heavy industry used the canal more as a refuse pit than as transportation. As the sludge increased, so did the smell. Contributed by tanneries, soap and cement factories, raw sewage combined to increase dangerous pollution levels. Soon, the oils and fumes rising to the top permeated the air, causing discoloration of the water—hence Lavender Lake.

In the 1880s, the *Brooklyn Eagle* labeled the canal an "open cesspool." In 1911, the Gowanus Flushing Tunnel was installed to help the tides circulate the waters. With a mechanical breakdown in the 1960s, the polluted canal became stagnated until community pressure forced the pump's rehabilitation.

Now all that is past. With the containerization of shipping, the port lost its industrial appeal, and the neighborhood turned to light industry.

Cormorant in Gowanus Canal. *Photo by John Manbeck.*

At the same time, community efforts to clean and rezone the area began. Warehouses and former factories have been renovated as cooperatives and studios. New office space has been taken by John Muir's Brooklyn Center for the Urban Environment, the Gowanus Canal Development Corporation and other environmental groups, including the Gowanus Dredgers Canoe Club and the Urban Divers. Fish also returned to the canal, as evidenced by cormorant fishing birds in the vicinity. In 2007, a pilot whale found its way into the canal.

History is deeply embedded in the neighborhood. The initial Battle of Brooklyn (1776) was fought on the banks of Gowanus Creek near the Old Stone House. In the mid-nineteenth century, the Brooklyn Superbas (later the Dodgers) played baseball in Washington Park that stood there. The wood-planked Carroll Street Bridge (1889), the oldest of four remaining retractile drawbridges or "swing bridges" in the country, still carries traffic and pedestrians. It replaced an 1887 wooden bridge and was landmarked in 1987 and reconstructed for its centennial on September 9, 1989.

Subsequently, other bridges crossed the canal as Gowanus developed into a residential and industrial location. In 1903, the Ninth Street Bridge

Carroll Street Bridge. *Photo by John Manbeck.*

opened, and two more bridges appeared in 1905—the Union Street Bridge and the Third Street Bridge. It wasn't until 1940 that the last two bridges opened with the construction of the Gowanus Expressway. The Hamilton Avenue Bridge (1942) and the Gowanus Canal Railroad Bridge, for the Ninth Street F-Line station, loom high over the canal. This F-Line stop stands eighty-seven feet above the canal at Smith and Ninth Streets, the highest station in the New York City transit system.

Developing faster than the neighboring port of Red Hook, Gowanus has a Whole Foods and three hotels operating: Comfort Inn, Hotel Le Bleu and Holiday Inn Express, with a fourth proposed. The movement for rezoning the district from industrial to residential has been promoted—albeit with community opposition—with the September announcement by Toll Brothers to build Gowanus Village, which will house 447 units in two twelve-story buildings.

But even with the protests, Gowanus will no longer remain a sleepy, irrelevant Brooklyn outpost. Online, there's the Gowanus Lounge, a newsy gossip blog, and the Gowanus Yacht Club has become a popular nightspot. This never would have been possible years ago.

Lavender has been colorized "red hot."

Williamsburg and My Grandfather, the Reporter

January 29 and February 5, 2009

One hundred years ago this year, my grandfather died of tuberculosis, contracted from his work on newspapers, including the *Brooklyn Times*. He died when my mother turned six. As a staff reporter, he covered breaking news, wrote features and reviewed theatrical performances. His name was John Cahill. In his papers, I found yellowing copies of his writing typed on legal-size paper with his penciled corrections, cross-outs and additions. Included with the news stories were a few creative pieces, possibly intended for features but maybe for a literary submission. One was a ghost story.

I thought it would be fun to put John Cahill in print again in a Brooklyn newspaper. Following is one of his stories about the changes in Williamsburg after the new bridge opened in 1903. He discusses the evolutionary changes as Brooklyn annexed adjacent towns, the original Dutch settlements and the City of Williamsburgh into what was then called the Eastern District, adding them to the City of Brooklyn in the 1850s.

In his language, Cahill reveals a suspicion that accompanied an upheaval of an older way of life. Before construction of the bridge, Williamsburg boasted a neighborhood of rich, lavish architecture in which the Vanderbilts, Whitneys and Fisks lived comfortably. The uneasiness that settled on Brooklyn was founded in a prejudice against change, as developers altered the way of life and the poorer Lower East Side immigrants invaded the new borough. His writing style has a touch of the florid language common at the time. It was written about 105 years ago. I have left his original spelling and corrections. (Even though the Dutch spelling of "Williamsburgh" was no longer used after its consolidation into Brooklyn, Cahill stubbornly repeats it.)

At the time, Cahill lived at 250 Keap Street. He had no more than an elementary school education and was largely a self-educated son of an Irish immigrant from a large family.

THE PASSING OF WILLIAMSBURGH: THE DEMOLITION OF THE OLD CITY IS NOW IN PROGRESS, AND A NEW AND PROBABLY GREATER ONE IS BEING CREATED

Of the three communities that made up the City of Williamsburgh, two, many years ago, lost the imprint of their original settlers by the influx

of new races. Bushwick's German architecture, dress and tongue, and the Greenpoint Irish, went slowly and gently, but to the largest village, from whence the city took its name, was reserved a long secluded life, ending unexpectedly in what promises to be practical effacement.

For the fifty years following its consolidation with Brooklyn, Williamsburgh was a recluse, a maze of crooked streets strewn with crumbling structures that were sometimes farmhouses and occasionally of a pretentious colonial form. Although a great manufacturing district grew on the river front and Bushwick teemed with the multiple activities of a ghetto, it remained undisturbed. Before the new bridge to Delancy Street brought this forgotten city into communication with the western shore of the river, the natives cherished the hope that the bulk of the traffic would go to the Brownsville settlements.

The first shock came the day the bridge was opened to pedestrians, when wide-eyed East Siders filled the quiet streets, peering at the venerable wooden houses and driving bargains. The spacious lots went cheap at first, so unusual was an offer of cash to owners long accustomed to dispose of their real estate by exchange and small sums to boot. Soon a swarm of investors sent prices flying; in the space of a few months, every piece of property increased fifty to three hundred percent in value, and then followed the movement to establish a new Williamsburgh.

Of the one hundred and fifty buildings destroyed for the bridge, the majority was frame, with wide porches and pointed roofs, owned by descendants of old Dutch and North German families, and those still standing of this type were on plots that attracted speculators.

Huge tenements went up, each entailing the sacrifice of two of the old homesteads. The enormous profit in this enterprise demonstrated, a score of builders set to work this summer between Broadway and Metropolitan Avenue, eagerly paying $10,000 for land that had gone begging for $4,000. In a territory less than four blocks square, six of these tenements have arisen, eight are in course of construction and in two blocks of South Third Street, ten houses have been razed within the past month for the same purpose.

The Williamsburghers who would not sell viewed these great piles with dread and pity, dread of the class who were ordained to occupy them, and pity for any such as must endure this mode of living. The latter emotion, at least, they no longer feel, for an inspection has shown that the safeguards the law provides for the tenement dweller gives him sanitation, ventilation and conveniences far superior to that in the Williamsburghers' most comfortable domicile.

There is no doubt that ultimately every lot in the market that is of sufficient size will have its six-story tenement, for the demand for apartments is too great to allow the land to lie financially fallow under the incubus of a house that will not accommodate at the crowding point more than three families. As the bridge has made Williamsburgh virtually a part of the East Side, it seems only a question of time when the transformation in inhabitants will be accomplished.

A minor influence that has been at work for the past decade is the abandonment of the neighborhood by the wealthy classes. The mansions of the Mayors [as a former city, Williamsburg would have had its own city hall] *and prominent citizens of the 70's are given over to boarding-house keepers and to clubs.*

Mayor [William] *Wall's fine old house on South Ninth Street has been converted into a cheap flat, and the homes of Mayors* [Abraham] *Berry and* [James] *Howell on the block above are each let to several families. Little slips of paper pasted on the door-jambs announce that furnished rooms may be had in the massive brownstone fronts that line what was in times gone by fashionable Bedford Avenue.*

Notwithstanding that seven of the Protestant churches have lost or will lose their edifices by condemnation or sale and are not building new ones in the vicinity, the remaining congregations feel the shift in population so severely that several are considering consolidation and others are going to new fields in the suburbs.

Within a few months, three public improvements will remove more of Williamsburgh. Roebling Street from South Fourth Street to Union Avenue will be widened an additional twenty feet, involving the destruction of sixty houses; Grand Street will be extended from South Fourth and Havemeyer Streets to Hooper Street, for which seventy-five pieces will be acquired by the city, including a church and school; and Montrose Avenue will be broken through from Union Avenue to Broadway. In addition to this, agents of the Metropolitan Railway Company and the Pennsylvania Railroad are negotiating for the entire block on the north of the bridge plaza. [In those days, rail transportation was privately owned and operated.]

South of Division Avenue, which once marked the boundary between Williamsburgh and Brooklyn, the path of the house-wrecker is an even broader one. The Eastern District Branch of the Y.M.C.A., just completed, took the best half of the block at Marcy Avenue and South Ninth Street, on the corner of which was Calvary Church; the Williamsburgh Library, opened last year, occupies the sites of another square of old houses, and

Williamsburg Bridge, 1903. Photo by A. Loeffler. *Courtesy of Marilyn Blaisdell.*

last week the tearing down of forty brick and brownstone structures for the Eastern District High School was completed.

In this locality, which has of late been included in the term Williamsburgh, the aristocracy once resided. Nowadays many of the houses are divided among three or four families, and others are let to lodgers. The few that still are tenanted by the original owners or their heirs will go for the more elaborate approaches to the Williamsburgh bridge, namely, the proposed Bedford Avenue extension and the broadening of Roebling Street south of Broadway. The latter will increase the width of the thoroughfare to eighty feet, beginning at Broadway and terminating at Taylor Street, about four blocks in all. Roebling Street houses are all small brick affairs, of a recent period, and not of any especial sentimental or pecuniary value.

The Bedford Avenue extension, however, will create so much havoc that an association of the residents made desperate efforts to defeat it. Upon being appealed to Comptroller Grout [Edward Grout, Brooklyn's first borough president], who spent his boyhood in the neighborhood, disappointed the association by championing the project for the bridge outlet and pushing it vigorously until it was passed by the Board of Estimate last February.

The extension will necessitate the creation of a new street, one hundred feet wide, running obliquely from Bedford Avenue and Heyward Street to Broadway and Havemeyer Street. More than a hundred fine residences, the First Baptist Church and part of the United Congregational Church will *disappear, and the new avenue, which will be a link in a direct highway from the Long Island farms to Wallabout Market, is expected to be a business street that will in time alter the district surrounding it.*

—*John L. Cahill*

The Art of Williamsburg
July 31, 2008

Art in Williamsburg has made great strides. In fact, all Williamsburg has progressed undoubtedly because of its attraction to artists. Much of the credit must be placed on the doorstep of the director of the Williamsburg Art & Historical Center, Yuko Nii. The center operates out of the former Kings County Savings Bank Building (1867) and celebrated an infusion of a $500,000 capital funding grant from the city.

Farther west, the Brooklyn Brewery has opened its summer doors for special events. Every Sunday, the brewery sponsors tours and gives history lessons on beer. No exams, though.

But it wasn't always like this. These are just two of the institutions that are brightening up the local scene. Movie festivals, clubs and boutiques also add to the nightlife. This current revolution can easily match the ones in 1903, when the Williamsburg Bridge opened, or 1954, when the BQE split the neighborhood in two. Williamsburg had been known as the Eastern District because it was east of the City of Brooklyn, along with Bushwick and Greenpoint. Other areas were Western Brooklyn (Flatbush and Bay Ridge) and South Brooklyn (Gowanus).

Like Carroll Gardens, Williamsburg was named after an individual who never lived in Brooklyn. Colonel Jonathan Williams, a surveyor, mapped the Cripplebush waterfront but lived in Philadelphia, as he was also a grandnephew of Benjamin Franklin.

Williamsburgh (with the "h") grew rapidly, with ferry service to Manhattan and a distillery, and incorporated as a city in 1827. In 1840, Williamsburgh was segregated from Bushwick. Then, in 1852, it was chartered as a city. Its independence was short-lived, for the City of Brooklyn annexed it in 1855 and cut off its "h."

The rich, many of whom had profitable industries by the river, flooded Williamsburg in the latter half of the nineteenth century. Lavish mansions with ornate architecture spread throughout the section as the Vanderbilts, Fisks and Whitneys moved there.

Then came the Williamsburg Bridge. The wealthy residents left as the working class crossed from Delancy Street to Broadway. The mansions turned into rooming houses. Workers from Astral Oil, Brooklyn Flint Glass, Havermeyer & Elder Sugar Company, Pfizer Pharmaceutical Company, Farberware and Helca Iron Works moved in and built their own more modest homes.

By 1937, Williamsburg Houses became one of the city's first housing projects. But when Robert Moses cut the BQE through Williamsburg, the neighborhood became even more fractured. Italians and Poles moved into Northside; Hassidic Jews bought up Southside; and Puerto Ricans stayed in Los Sures, or Spanish Southside. In addition, there was Cripplebush and Newtown Creek.

Many streets are named after signers of the Declaration of Independence, so there's a good history lesson in Williamsburg. Look for Hews Street and Keap Street. (What? You can't find a Keap among the signers? Try Thomas McKean, who our city fathers thought was Thomas M. Keap. Look carefully!) Even a 1906 statue of George Washington sits on his horse at Washington Plaza, a former terminus of trolley cars. But Roebling Street, nowhere near the Brooklyn Bridge or its creator's home, leads off the Williamsburg Bridge.

Hungry? Try Diner at 85 Broadway and Berry Street. (Abraham Berry was a former mayor of the City of Williamsburgh.) It's rated high for its American-French fare at "popular prices." Something sweet? How about the soda fountain at the Savoy Sweet Shop, 451 Broadway? And there's always Peter Luger's Steakhouse at 178 Broadway; if you need a menu, you don't belong there. (In 1876, it was known as Charlie Luger's Café, Billiards and Bowling Alley. In those days, that meant, "Women not allowed.")

So Williamsburg is another one of Brooklyn's "in" neighborhoods that are luring so many new residents and hipsters to Billyburg. But then we know that Brooklyn always was the "in" place, historically speaking. Now everyone is in on the secret.

Tales of Manhattan Beach
August 7 and 14, 2008

Over recent years, Manhattan Beach has felt the Russian influx and has changed. McMansions now fill building lots, with older houses being demolished for newer behemoths. No longer are there vacant lots on

Oriental Boulevard. Pembroke Street, which had been residences for naval and coast guard military, has been swallowed by Kingsborough Community College. But the beach, still small and protected in a cove, remains popular and well kept by the parks department.

When did Manhattan Beach become popular? Initially, what is now Coney Island was not much more than a large elongated sandbar. Lowlifes lived in the western end. Just like Long Island, the rich congregated on the eastern tip. But then the *vox populi* descended on Coney, and the rich departed. They left their two hotels that give their names to the area: the Manhattan and the Oriental.

But by the end of World War I, a new owner, real estate auctioneer Joseph Day, managed Manhattan Beach and all oceanfront property to Coney Island Avenue. Austin Corbin, the former owner of the hotels, had died in 1896, and his college-aged son had failed to keep the income flowing. Day knew what to do: tear down the hotels and divide the real estate into lots and sell to developers. Don't we still do that?

Day demolished the hotels and then established Manhattan Beach Estates in the 1920s. As a lure, he also created Manhattan Beach Baths and Brighton Beach Baths. That way, average, middle-class people could visit, rent a cabana for the summer months and enjoy the neighborhood, see the choice real estate and buy. His demand for all developers in Manhattan Beach: glamorize the property.

Street names were Anglicized to reflect British upper-class taste. His design for the community emphasized the romantic and hid the mundane. Service areas for sanitation collection and deliveries were located in alleys behind houses (since eliminated), and utility poles remained hidden in the back of lots. The first private home on Manhattan Beach appeared on Falmouth Street in 1909 and was of "Moorish design."

Initially, during Corbin's reign, the hotels and private beaches served high rollers at the Sheepshead Bay Race Track and the old rich nobility. But hard times created by a crash caused fallout of interest in horse racing. Then New York State passed anti-betting legislation, and the three Gravesend tracks closed in 1911. The hotels followed. The Oriental, initially used as offices by Day, was taken down in 1916 to become planking for the boardwalk and bungalows of Rockaway Point across Jamaica Bay.

Day announced his first plans for Manhattan Beach Estates: 114 new homes complete with sewers, sidewalks, water, gas and electricity. Utilities were to be hidden under an easement running behind the houses. To demonstrate that the development would not be abandoned, he started the

Manhattan Beach Bath Houses and Resort on the site of the Oriental Hotel, near today's beach. It had handball courts for exercise, a pool for children and a popular singer, Rudy Vallee, for entertainment in the 1921 season. Interestingly, dancing was not permitted. The cost for a summer season pass was twenty dollars. To show his confidence, Day purchased one of the nine original houses built on Corbin Place.

Manhattan Beach houses didn't sell briskly. When compared to the original 1876 purchase price for the entire peninsula—$16,500 for five hundred acres of unimproved shorefront property—the price of houses costing $9,000 to $15,000 was hardly a bargain. Bungalows were the first houses built on West End Avenue. Lots were then laid out on Amherst, Exeter, Beaumont, Falmouth, Hastings, Jaffrey, Kensington, Langham and Mackenzie Streets. But a mild depression hit in the early 1920s.

The real estate lull didn't last long, though. In 1925, a building boom struck. The Blackstone Hotel, on Oriental Boulevard and West End Avenue, which had been on the market for a year, sold for $1 million. Blocks of houses sold quickly. The Long Island Rail Road, which operated the Manhattan Beach line directly to the hotel, announced that it would discontinue the spur in 1924. In 1941, the station property and right-of-way from Neptune Avenue to Oriental Boulevard was sold to the Trump Brighton Corp. for $175,000. (This was Fred Trump, Donald's father.) But the Plum Beach Auto Stage Co. operated a bus into Sheepshead Bay for ten cents, so Manhattan Beach residents were not inconvenienced.

Then the entertainers arrived to raise the ante and lure the customers. The tradition stemmed from the band concerts of the 1880s. After the Civil War, the world immersed itself in music with patriotic concerts and operatic performances. Soloists turned into pop stars with fans following them from one concert to another. This musical world heralded a new age for musical appreciation that had previously been limited to the parlor piano. Manhattan Beach and Brighton Beach had been outposts for conductors Patrick Gilmore, John Philip Sousa ("The Manhattan Beach March"), Arthur Pryor, Victor Herbert and Anton Siedl. Now, in the 1920s, Joseph Day revived and modernized the attractions.

On the Manhattan Beach bandstand, Paul Whiteman, Ted Lewis and Ben Bernie welcomed Mayors John Hylan and James J. Walker to the breezy shore. Celebrities from the nascent film industry at Brooklyn's Vitagraph Studios—John Bunny, Francis X. Bushman, Clara Bow and producer Adolph Zukor—relaxed at Manhattan Beach just as politicians and horse racing aficionados had decades earlier.

Comedian Henry Morgan broadcasting from Manhattan Beach Baths in the 1930s. Photo by Herman Field. *Kingsborough Historical Society.*

The popularity of Day's resort grew so rapidly that he needed to make changes. In 1927, rocks from the Empire State Building excavation in New York filled the eastern coastline, and Oriental Beach opened. A new Rainbow Bandshell replaced the old bandstand when the Oriental's lagoon was filled. Year-round entertainment after the Manhattan Beach Lodge opened spiked the sale of over twenty-five thousand memberships. On Sundays, even in mid-winter, the gate recorded ten thousand admissions.

In 1935, when swing and "truckin'" popularized the dance floors, dance bands rotated appearances at Manhattan Beach. Les Brown, Artie Shaw, Benny Goodman, Tommy Dorsey, Guy Lombardo, Kay Kyser, Ina Ray Hutton and even Louis Prima came to "play pretty for the people." New artists performed along with established stars, and many of them were Brooklyn-born: Alice Faye, Danny Kaye, Buddy Hackett, Phil Silvers, Bob Hope, Tallulah Bankhead and Helen Hayes. Mayor Fiorello LaGuardia dropped by. NBC sent its new television cameras over to film a tennis match in 1939. Occasionally, an itinerant disc jockey from WMCA broadcast new recorded songs from the southern Brooklyn location.

The baths boasted a baseball diamond, two outdoor pools, a skating rink (both roller and ice), miniature golf, basketball, tennis and handball courts, a calisthenics program and a restaurant. Manhattan Beach resident Herman

Field photographed the action. Female lifeguards graced the cover of *Life* magazine with the accompanying headlines, "Life Goes to a Party at Joseph Day's Manhattan Beach Baths." The resort was billed as the "World's Largest Privately Owned Playground."

By 1939, over in the residential market, 88 new houses rose on Manhattan Beach, as well as 174 summer cottages. The year 1940 saw a similar growth, and by 1941, the Waxboro Corporation developers advertised a home community on eastern Manhattan Beach for $4 million. The neighborhood attracted much new blood.

But on December 7, 1941, when Johnny McGee, the bandleader playing at the Manhattan Beach Baths Lodge, announced the bombardment of Pearl Harbor, the resort began a drastic re-evaluation. No longer would the peninsula be a summertime playground in Brooklyn. Now it would be a training ground for war.

Within a month, members were told to clean out their lockers and that a new landlord controlled Manhattan Beach—the U.S. government.

Vanished Neighborhoods
April 5, 2005

Ghost neighborhoods existed on maps early in the populating of Brooklyn, but they have since been absorbed into larger entities, forgotten or outdated. While their designations are considered obsolete, here are a few that were familiar "once upon a time."

Plunders Neck: This peninsula in New Lots borders on the waters that once attracted pirates and other unworthies who plundered. With Spring Creek to the east, Betts Creek to the west and Jamaica Bay to the south, fishermen and farmers who built wooden frame houses for themselves joined the underworld there. Once the criminal element left, a hotel rose at Forbell's Landing near Mill Pond. Now the neighborhood is famous for the Louis H. Pink housing project and the Pitkin Avenue subway yards.

City Line: This east central community was named when Brooklyn existed as an independent city. The neighborhood bordered the line between Brooklyn and Nassau County (later the Borough of Queens). With its diverse population and name changes, the only remnant of the original designation is the City Line Cinema.

Crow Hill: The Crow Hill neighborhood ran from eastern Prospect Park to East New York. According to an 1873 issue of the *Brooklyn Eagle*, the name derived from a large number of crows roosting on the large hill in the area. Another opinion, derogatory in origin, claimed that the name came from a community of African Americans who lived there in shanties in the 1830s, working in the fish and meat markets. In 1846, the Kings County Penitentiary opened its gates on the crest of the hill as part of the group of county buildings there. In 1907, the prison was demolished, as the residential neighborhood grew and Brooklyn Preparatory School replaced it. Today, Medgar Evers College occupies the site. The community was renamed Crown Heights, retaining the same initials. Ironically, a new development named Crow Hill is being constructed near Eastern Parkway.

South Brooklyn: This is the neighborhood south of the original City of Brooklyn—not Coney Island. The district was named in 1855 and includes the later neighborhoods of Gowanus, Red Hook, Carroll Gardens, Park Slope and the Columbia Street Waterfront District.

Eastern District: Collectively, this district encompasses the communities in the northeast of Brooklyn—Williamsburg, Bushwick and Greenpoint—after they were annexed by the City of Brooklyn in 1855. The term distinguished them from the Western District of South Brooklyn and Flatbush. The last vestige of the term disappeared when Eastern District High School closed in 1998.

Part VII

HOLIDATES

Birthday Precedents
February 17, 2011

Next Monday we will celebrate Presidents Day. Is this a generic holiday or one possessed by ALL presidents, past and future? (Note the lack of an apostrophe.) Or does it solely belong to the two presidents whose birthdays frame the date: Lincoln (the 12th) and Washington (the 22nd)?

But this was not always so. And there have been precedents. The *Brooklyn Daily Eagle* of yore (available online from the Brooklyn Public Library) recorded more solemn and celebratory occasions. While we regard these auspicious occasions as clarions to shop, centuries ago, only random sales items peeked from the pages of the *Eagle*, such as an advertisement for "ice cream bricks" and an announcement that a clothing shop would be open on Washington's Birthday. By 1902, shoppers could buy boxes of candy decorated with tri-cornered hats and "ferocious looking hatchets" for ten cents. However, the Mercantile Library closed for half a day after noon in 1862. Rather, the birthday was celebrated with a commemoration—a "grand military, fancy dress and civic ball" in 1858 at Musical Hall at the corner of Fulton and Orange Streets, and the Brooklyn City Armory was illuminated by members of the Fourteenth Regiment.

By 1879, the patriotic gatherings made page 4 with the 147th celebration of Washington's birth at the Brooklyn Institute located on Washington

Final Fireman's Parade at the Washington Day Parade at Borough Hall in 1941. *Brooklyn Public Library, Brooklyn Collection.*

Street. Among the decorations were the president's portrait and Francis Guy's painting *Water Street*. However, the speech given by the Reverend Charles Hall dealt with "Patrick Henry, the Patriot and Orator."

In 1891, the Navy Yard commandant closed the base for the day but ordered ships dressed in "rainbow form" and a twenty-one-gun salute at noon. The Volunteer Firemen's Association celebrated in 1894 with a sunrise one-hundred-gun salute in Fort Greene, followed by its annual parade from Carroll Street to Henry, Remsen and Brooklyn City Hall. "One sees a wider variety of styles of beard than at any other meeting of the year," the reporter wrote about the firemen. "The modern foppish mustache finds scant favor among them, and the good, sturdy old American chin whisker which fairly bristles with character and stubbornness predominates." Usually, the fire wagon had portraits of Washington on its flanks.

The celebration of Washington's birthday as a holiday was enacted by Congress in 1880. It was originally celebrated only in the District of Columbia but was later expanded as a federal holiday in 1885. The date marked the first federal holiday to honor an American citizen. But the problem with this anniversary is the date. Washington's birth date, February 22, 1732, is recorded in the Gregorian calendar, but that wasn't implemented by England until 1752. According to the Julian calendar, which was in use at the time of Washington's birth, he was born on February 11, 1731, one year and one week earlier. Shouldn't we celebrate Presidents Day on that day?

This brings us to Lincoln. The *Eagle* reported that Lincoln celebrated Washington's birthday in 1861 at Independence Hall in Philadelphia, where he cited the Declaration of Independence as the savior of the country, wondering—on the brink of the Civil War—"how this country can be saved upon this basis." Of course, both men had visited Brooklyn—Washington at the Battle of Brooklyn in 1776 and Lincoln in 1860 before he delivered his Cooper Union speech.

Lincoln's birth date is a bit clearer: February 12, 1809. It is a legal holiday in some states, including New York, New Jersey and Connecticut, a situation that was remedied with the Presidents Day celebration. No federal holiday honors Lincoln. The earliest observation of his birthday occurred in Buffalo in 1874.

The *Eagle* records veterans' celebrations in the 1890s with dinners and parades. Since the day was a legal holiday in New York, schools and banks were closed. By 1897, with the Civil War only thirty-two years in the past, veterans gave tribute to Lincoln with reunions, banquets and parades. The following year, an annual food show capitalized on the day with patriotic decorations. Other organizations, the Trinity Club and the Cortelyou Club, joined with dinners and special entertainment.

In 1899, Plymouth Church, Henry Ward Beecher's former parish, hosted a meeting "in the interest of negro industrial education" in an attempt to continue the work of Lincoln. Among the speakers was Booker T. Washington of the Tuskegee Institute. Then, in 1900, an ad in the *Eagle* promoted "Lincoln's Birthday Delightful Sea Trips to Washington, D.C." on the steamship *Old Point Comfort*. Round-trip fare (including meals and stateroom accommodations) was fifteen dollars.

Today, we celebrate Presidents Day with the guarantee that it will not fall on either of the February birthdays of our most honored chief executives. How's that for a precedent?

Anniversary of the *Vin Fiz* Flight

September 22, 2011

Just in case you missed it, the *Vin Fiz* took off from Sheepshead Bay last week bound for Long Beach, California, on the first solo transcontinental flight. The date was September 17, 1911. The news may have been a bit slow in getting to you, what with storms and anniversaries, but it certainly was a headline-making event.

Those with calculators will be able to figure out that this year—2011—was the centennial of that flight. So why was there no celebration or parade or even reference to it in Brooklyn? Ask Borough Hall. Ask the borough president. Ask Marty (www.brooklyn-usa.org).

Certainly the federal government knew about it. In the Smithsonian Institution is a re-creation of the Wright brothers' plane and a major display in the National Air and Space Museum in Washington, D.C. This historic flight took place eight years after the Wright brothers flew 852 feet at Kitty Hawk. The pilot of the *Vin Fiz* was Calbraith Perry Rodgers. His flight to California was 4,321 miles, which he covered in eighty-two hours.

I wrote about the centennial three years ago, alerting Brooklynites to the event. Here's a recap of the facts. And they all started in Brooklyn.

Years ago, three racetracks existed in Brooklyn, the oldest and most elite being the Sheepshead Bay Race Track, founded by Leonard Jerome, August Belmont and William Vanderbilt. The racing season ran from late spring through late August, with meets circulating among the Kings County parks and up to Morris Park in the Bronx and out to Monmouth in New Jersey. When the tracks were not used for racing, they were rented out for other events such as military reviews, concerts, parades and, in 1911, as an airstrip.

Rodgers was a big, fearless man who stood at six feet, four inches and had been a football player. Three of his ancestors had been commodores in the American Navy. The plane he flew, constructed from cloth over a wooden frame, was commissioned from the Wright brothers. It was a biplane mounted with double fuel tanks and a four-cylinder, thirty-five-horsepower, water-cooled engine capable of a top speed of sixty-five miles per hour.

The name of the plane, *Vin Fiz*, was the sponsor of the flight, a carbonated grape drink produced by Armour, the meatpacking company. Rodgers not only had the wings and fuselage painted with their logo but he also tied a bottle of the drink to the plane's strut for good luck. The bottle survived all fifteen crashes.

Calbraith Rodgers taking off from Sheepshead Bay, 1911. *Smithsonian Institution, National Air and Space Museum.*

On the afternoon of September 17, the paying crowds and the pilot were ready for the flight that crystallized aviation as viable transportation. Rodgers, stuffed into a seat mounted on the fuselage (no cockpit) wore a leather vest lined with newspapers for warmth and leather boots. His wife, Mabel, had sewn corduroy on the seat so he wouldn't slide out of the plane. With no cabin, the pilot flew at the mercy of the elements.

Strapped to the fuselage was a mailbag, now at the Smithsonian. It cost twenty-five cents extra to send letters on this first airmail flight. With his cap reversed, Rodgers donned his goggles, lit his cigar and climbed onto the wooden fuselage. "Let 'er go!" he yelled. Taking off from the Sheepshead Bay Race Track, he edged the plane through and over the cheering crowd and then "drove" to Coney Island, circled it and flew over Flatbush Avenue at eight hundred feet. At the Brooklyn Navy Yard, he flew past the battleship *Connecticut*, over the Brooklyn Bridge, up Broadway and along Twenty-third Street in Manhattan and on to Jersey City, where his wife, his mother, a three-man crew and an equipment train complete with replacement parts awaited him.

From Jersey City, he followed the "iron compass" (railroad tracks) to Middletown, New York, but the flight plans were not as smooth from then on. In all, Rodgers had sixty-eight takeoffs and crashed nineteen times. By the end of the trip, only one original rudder and the strut that the bottle of Vin Fiz was attached to survived. Finally, in Pasadena, California, he was wrapped in an American flag as a victory symbol. He discussed his plans for a transoceanic flight to England sixteen years before Charles Lindbergh flew solo across the Atlantic.

Five months after his record-breaking flight, Rodgers took a warm-up flight, dipped over the roller coaster on the Long Beach Pier and flew into a flock of frightened seagulls. One bird jammed the controls, and the *Vin Fiz* crashed for the final time into the sea, killing Cal Rodgers on April 4, 1912. His epitaph reads, "I endure, I conquer." In 1986, a re-enactment of Rodgers's flight by James Lloyd covered the same route—without the accidents.

Today's airport in Long Beach, California, has a tribute to the bravery and the end of Cal Rodgers and his first transcontinental flight. Brooklyn, where he started, should do no less.

Part VIII

HARD TIMES

The Great Depression in Brooklyn
November 20, 2008

As the financial walls tumble around our ankles in 2008, our thoughts eerily return to "Black Tuesday" and "Black Thursday" in October 1929. How was Brooklyn affected by the oncoming Great Depression? Can we see parallels?

Of course, seventy-nine years ago, a different scenario materialized, as few of today's "safeguards" had been enacted. Still, America stood firmly on the gold standard back then, which affected Europe's economy. What happened over here turned into a global crisis. A "bank holiday" closed savings institutions for four days. That hasn't happened this year—yet. Brooklyn found its voice after having been reduced to a borough in 1898. Downtown development on Fulton Street boasted new department store buildings for Abraham & Straus (now Macy's), Loeser's and Namm's. Brooklyn's tallest building, the Williamsburgh Savings Bank building, affectionately known as "Willie," opened in 1929. So did the Flatbush movie emporium, Loew's Kings and, out in Coney Island, the Half Moon Hotel, with pretensions of returning to the glory days of the gigantic 1890s caravansaries.

Among the new products on grocery shelves were Wonder Bread and Mott's applesauce. Windshield wipers appeared on cars as an option, while overhead flew the new airships from American Airlines and Trans-World Airlines (TWA). Pinball machines turned into a new vice for teenagers.

Oh, yes. In October 1929, the *Brooklyn Eagle* ran a story about a gasoline shortage—caused by a strike of delivery drivers. Then the stock market crashed. Over the next few weeks, stock market indicators bobbed up and down on a roller-coaster binge. The Republican president, Herbert Hoover, reported that the economy was "solid" after a $15 billion loss during the first week.

Newspapers wrote about suicides and an increase in crime, particularly robberies, including one at the Navy Yard and another at the Flatbush Savings Bank. While new housing developments opened in Dyker Heights, construction on the whole was down and foreclosures up. Even the *Eagle* raised its price to a dime. With jobs scarce and soup lines more apparent, immigration cracked down and deported Mexican workers (presumably undocumented). As usual, race was an issue. "Hoovervilles," sometimes called "Pigtowns," proliferated in Brooklyn and across the country. Mysterious forces shot gangster Jack "Legs" Diamond for trying to break into Brooklyn's beer racket.

But escapism remedied some of the gloom, as Brooklyn theaters featured films that "talked" accompanied by stage shows and personal appearances of bandleader Cab Calloway at the Albee, singer Rudy Vallee at the Brooklyn Paramount and actress Jean Harlow at the Loew's Metropolitan. Brooklyn's World War I veterans marched against Hitler's treatment of the Jews in Europe.

By 1932, a new president moved into the White House, but the Depression had become a permanent part of Americans' lives. FDR closed the banks for a week so they could recoup, but soup lines increased. Down in Washington, the Senate opened an investigation. Hard times prevailed in Brooklyn and in the rest of the world until World War II introduced other problems.

I'm not sure how many parallels you can find, but obviously we haven't learned too much over time. That's what history demonstrates. Does history repeat itself? This time, though, we don't have the Marx brothers playing on the stage of the Brooklyn Loew's Metropolitan to make the gloom disappear.

Both are gone.

WPA in Brooklyn
March 5, 2009

Federal works projects stimulate the economy by strengthening the infrastructure of the country through employment. With this impetus, the country profits through construction of roads, bridges and other public projects. It happened during the Great Depression, 1929–40, and President Obama has promised to reinvigorate our current economic situation with similar acts.

The goals of the New Deal in the 1930s also addressed environmental and cultural lapses with the Civilian Conservation Corps (CCC), National Recovery Act (NRA) and the Works Progress Administration (WPA). The first worked on national parks and similar projects, while the latter created theatrical, artistic and literary projects.

The Federal Writers Project reinvigorated a failing Broadway, encouraged new outlets and introduced new talents such as writer Richard Wright and artist Reginald Marsh. While most of the program's beneficiaries are gone, at least one remnant of the age remains: the murals they created. Many appear in post offices and other federal buildings, but their influence seeped down to the local level, carrying over to public works sponsored by the cities and states in schools, libraries and housing projects. The central building of the Brooklyn Public Library at Grand Army Plaza has two: *Children with Sheep* (1938) by Thomas Saviano and *Bear* (1936) by Edna Gluck. At Brooklyn's Federal Courthouse at 225 Cadman Plaza East, *The Role of the Immigrant in the Industrial Development of America* (1937) by Edward Laning can be found in Courtroom 3. Originally, it had adorned Ellis Island. One can only hope that deportees are not processed in that room. WPA artists decorated several buildings and reliefs of the Prospect Park Zoo, including the Elephant House, the Monkey House and the Lion House, all in 1935.

Brooklyn schools also benefitted from these commissions. Repositories of WPA artwork include Brooklyn Technical High School with *History of Mankind in Terms of Mental and Physical Labor* (1941) by Maxwell Starr; Erasmus High School with *Wanderings of Ulysses—Homer's World* (1939) by Nato Receputo; George Westinghouse Vocational and Technical High School with *Workers in a Foundry* (1939) by Rudolph Henn; and in Music Room 327 of Abraham Lincoln High School, *Primitive Music and Religious and Modern Music* (1937) by Seymour Fogel.

Other Brooklyn secondary schools that have WPA artwork include Franklin K. Lane, Midwood, Prospect Heights, Samuel Tilden, Sarah J. Hale Technical and William E. Grady Career and Technical. At least three elementary schools also have examples of Depression-era art. Both Red Hook and Williamsburg federal housing projects possess other WPA artwork. For details on these federal works, see www.wpamurals.com/newyork.htm. What do not appear on the website are two controversial murals that were removed for political reasons from Brooklyn Borough Hall and Floyd

Bennett Field, now Gateway National Recreation Area. Conservative watch groups perceived installations at both locations as subversive Communist propaganda.

In Borough Hall, two murals titled *Brooklyn Past and Present* (1939), painted by twenty-five-year-old Valois Fabry Jr., depicted three centuries of Brooklyn history. The two-year project had been dedicated by Borough President Raymond Ingersoll, according to a 2006 *New York Times* column by Leonard Bernardo and Jennifer Weiss, but was removed in 1946 by his successor, John Cashmore. Because of a "Lenin-like" figure hidden among the crowds, the offending mural was stored in the top floor of Borough Hall but may have been destroyed during the building's 1980s renovation.

At Floyd Bennett Field, then a city-owned commercial airport, three of four WPA murals by August Henkel were removed from the administration building, according to a 1940 article in *Time*. The fate of the fourth mural is unexplained. The New York City WPA administrator, Lieutenant Colonel Brehon Somervell, ordered them burned because an image of the Soviet leader, Josef Stalin, was inserted in the painting. The artist, who had run for Congress under the Communist Party ticket when it was still legal, claimed the offending subject to be an Austrian parachutist named Franz Reichelt, although he couldn't explain the red star painted on the Floyd Bennett hangar. Maybe it was a Macy's star, suggested Geoffrey Hellman of the *New Yorker*.

Recently, Gateway announced a complete restoration of the Floyd Bennett Administration Building to its 1930s design. Perhaps National Parks could restore the WPA murals as well.

New York Dock Company
May 19, 2011

As Brooklyn Bridge Park readies for another season with fundraising parties, a bicycle marathon and an open house with free games, we notice the verdant new shrubbery, the stirrings of the contractors at work and three new large solar storage trucks.

Cormorants vie with seagulls and families of ducks for the new supplies of seafood as bikers vie with runners and dog walkers on the paths. Soon, the newly delivered trees and bushes will be planted, and the bridge from Squibb Park will be snaking down to the park. Can spring really be here finally?

New York Dock Company headquarters on Furman and Joralemon Streets. *Photo by John Manbeck.*

Yet vestiges of yesteryear still lurk in corners of this once-busy port of Brooklyn. It's difficult to realize that the New York Dock Company that operated the Brooklyn (and New York) waterfront managed the piers and waterways of the East River as well as those of Atlantic and Erie Basins in Red Hook, bordering Bush Terminal in Sunset Park. A reminder of a New York Dock Company building stands at the edge of the park at Joralemon and Furman Streets emblazoned with the date 1917. Near Pier 1, tracks for the industrial railway and former truck beds are exposed.

The New York Dock Company stood huge and high, as New York's port was one of America's biggest and Brooklyn's harbor was one of the best. By 1900, the company consolidated property between Fulton Street (now Old Fulton Street) and Erie Basin. It owned miles of railroad tracks and sheds, over 40 piers and about 150 stores and warehouses and "massive gray loft buildings," according to the 1930's *WPA Guide to New York City*, which stated, "The small [shipping] lines...stack the bulkheads with cargoes from every port in the world." The company emerged as the largest private freight terminal in the world.

The waterfront had a different feeling then, one of industry, dirt and grime. Now the shipping industry has adapted to containerized commerce, and the scene has shifted to roomier New Jersey. However, Ernest Poole's 1915 novel *The Harbor* presents a vivid picture of life on the Brooklyn waterfront at the turn of the last century. It was a different Brooklyn and a sordid life on the East River.

The control of Brooklyn's waterways harks back to the formation of the City of Brooklyn in the 1830s. The City of New York had been opposed to the competition from the other side of the East River but realized that whoever controlled the commerce would rule both cities. New York maneuvered to command the waterways on both shores of the East River, thereby exerting power over ferry companies and commercial shipping. By the turn of the twentieth century, New York had become the busiest port in the world.

Today, remains of the New York Dock Company empire can be seen in Brooklyn near Pier 6 and in warehouses and office buildings in Red Hook at Atlantic Basin. In 1902, the *Eagle* cited stories of the company expanding for additional control of the waterfront. Opinions ran high that the company's ownership cancelled rights of the people, "effectively disposing of the public ownership of the water front under the Dongan charter, because it firmly establishes the New York Dock Company" as owners.

With the dissolution of the company, the Port of New York Authority developed in 1921, eventually to morph into the Port Authority of New York and New Jersey. Attitudes about water changed to images of sailboats and ferries. Fortunately, the abandoned docks below Brooklyn Heights grew into the city's beautiful Brooklyn Bridge Park over recent years, an oasis for environmental cleanliness rather than the heart of pollution and the shipping industry. Converted barges serving as the Bargemusic and River Café at the tip of Old Fulton Street bring the only thought of former shipping commerce to Brooklyn today.

Brooklyn's Disappearing Waterfront
July 2, 2010

Brooklyn's historic waterfront is fading into history, with its few remaining symbols disappearing. For the sake of Brooklyn Bridge Park, piers have been stripped to their foundations and their shores reshaped. The once-vibrant eight-mile shoreline ran from Greenpoint through Wallabout Bay to the Heights to Red Hook Point and then to the Atlantic Basin and Gowanus Bay. It was replete with piers, dry docks, grain elevators and factories and topped off with warehouses and ferry wharves. Many of these artifacts have been removed or converted to sections of the future park or the Brooklyn Cruise or Brooklyn Marine Terminals.

Now the most familiar shipping is the Water Taxi and the East River Ferry. Still surviving is the New York Dock Co. building (1917) at Furman and Joralemon, now the park's headquarters, and the converted apartments in the former 1861 Brooklyn City Railroad Company offices at Furman and Old Fulton Streets.

The most obvious shrinking edifice is the National Cold Storage building, which is being demolished floor by floor to be replaced by commercial enterprises. While the century-old warehouse was not particularly distinctive, it was immortalized in 1966 by poet Harvey Shapiro as symbolic of our national history. "Hard by the Brooklyn Bridge it stands," Shapiro wrote it in tribute to John Kennedy. "They fall into the National Cold Storage Company one by one...fed by everything—ships, poems, stars, all the years of our lives."

Shipping fed the warehouses and then the ferries, starting in the seventeenth century. By the following century, ferries became such a significant resource that the City of New York obtained possession of Brooklyn's waterfront so it could control the ferry traffic between the cities. The first ferry landing was at Livingston's Wharf at the foot of Joralemon Street. Ferries soon became the "Gateway to Brooklyn" with other ferry slips at Fulton Street (Old Ferry Road), Montague Street, Atlantic Avenue (South Ferry) and Hamilton Ferry on Columbia Street. Fulton introduced the steam-powered ferry in 1814, while the Wall Street Ferry opened in 1851.

The ferries became so successful that grandiose new ferry terminals for the Fulton Ferry and the Wall Street Ferry (at the foot of Montague Street) were built in 1871. In spite of the opening of the Brooklyn Bridge, ferries continued their popularity as bridge traffic became more popular and crowded. By 1899, the Brooklyn Heights Railroad ran cable cars for the half-mile along Montague Street from Court Street, under the Hicks Street Arch (with Montague Terrace above) and on to the Wall Street Ferry. The line met the Furman Street trolleys and was electrified in 1909. But the Wall Street Ferry stopped in 1909, so the Montague trolley cut back to Hicks Street. The Furman Street line closed in 1915.

Other piers joined the waterfront scenery, with freighters the primary trade and railroads shipping freight cars on barges from Brooklyn to New Jersey. Then the Port Authority assumed control of the New York and New Jersey waterfront. By 1973, a privately owned company had built sheds and rails next to the old Montague Street ferry slip until the Port Authority took command.

Henrik Krogius, in the *Brooklyn Daily Eagle*, wrote in June that the rail pier next to Pier 4 had been collapsing. A Skanska spokesperson reported that it was being "allowed to return to nature." On the map for Brooklyn Bridge Park, the section will be projected as a wildlife refuge and a calm-water boat basin named Nature Island and Pebble Beach.

So products of man's industrialization are slowly returning to nature. The construction of Brooklyn Bridge Park is assisting in the process, and throughout its creation, much is being recycled and helping to create a unique treasure.

Brooklyn's Weather Anomalies
October 28, 2010

Recent weather upheavals give us reason to examine weather patterns around Brooklyn throughout the centuries. The topic of discussion last month, specifically the "twin tornadoes" of September 16, has centered about the unusual event of that late afternoon. While Brooklyn, New York, is not in the path of "tornado alley" (however, Brooklyn, Iowa, is), we have endured newsworthy storms over the years. And that does not include the football team, Brooklyn Storm, or baseball's Brooklyn Cyclones.

Only several years ago, on August 8, 2007, Bay Ridge and Sunset Park were hit by a "freak" twenty-minute tornado that peeled roofs off houses and caused havoc among the tree population. Leaving Bay Ridge, the storm hopped over to Prospect Park South. While tornadoes have struck other sections of New York, the only predecessor in Brooklyn was a tornado that swept through on July 8, 1887.

The 2010 storm hit Park Slope and Prospect Heights and then moved to Dumbo, Fort Greene, Crown Heights, Clinton Hill, Bed-Stuy, Williamsburg and Greenpoint, decimating our park and street-tree population and wrecking a few cars along the way, causing outages, then continued on to Queens and Long Island, as reported in the pages of the *Brooklyn Daily Eagle*.

While tornados are rare, hurricanes are a more familiar weather threat. The big one of 1938 (September 21), commonly named the "Long Island Express" because of its impact on the island, hit Brooklyn's coastline, moving seawalls around Manhattan Beach, flooding basements in southern Brooklyn and killing ten New Yorkers. Charlie Pierce, a neophyte forecaster, predicted the danger of the storm but was overruled by his superiors. The Great Atlantic Hurricane of 1944 (September 14) broke wind records in New York City.

At that point, the weather service started naming hurricanes: Edna and Carol (1954), Connie and Diane (1955), Donna (1960), Esther (1961), Doria (1971), Agnes (1972), Belle (1976), Gloria (1985), Felix (1995), Bertha (1996), Edouard (1996), Floyd (1999), Isabel (2003), Frances (2004), Ernesto (2006) and Barry (2007). Most of these caused flooding in New York City but no other significant damage. The most deaths occurred from the 1938 storm.

But storms had hit the area before, particularly in the 1890s decade, when winter storms caused erosion along the Coney Island shore, toppling seaside hotels and amusements into the water. For example, on July 19, 1850, a hurricane destroyed a Coney Island bathhouse, and on October 13, 1896, a severe storm washed away the Brighton Beach Music Hall and the tip of the Iron Pier, a two-story shopping mall that extended into the ocean. A record tide flooded Coney Island on November 27, 1900, and a hurricane on November 25, 1950, damaged the Sheepshead Bay pedestrian bridge.

A list of hurricanes in Wikipedia cites the Great Storm of 1693 (October 29), which caused severe damage on Long Island, and a hurricane that struck New York City on August 19, 1788. On August 24, 1893, a hurricane struck the Rockaway Peninsula and then passed through Brooklyn. And on August 18, 1911, a bolt of lightning struck the Giant Coaster, a roller coaster in Brighton Beach. To protect the shoreline, the Army Corps of Engineers recommended a fifteen-foot wall running along Coney Island's beach. It was promptly ridiculed.

Another familiar winter storm has been the blizzard. The Blizzard of '88 (March 12, 1888) stands out as the one to beat, as it piled twenty-one inches of snow with up to thirty-foot drifts on the streets of Brooklyn before there was a sanitation department to dig us out. The recovery took fourteen days.

Winter storm at Brighton Beach, 1893. *Frank Leslie's Illustrated News.*

But the twentieth century also had its headline grabbers with a ten-inch snowfall on February 14, 1914. Just before Christmas in 1947, a blizzard closed Brooklyn's surface transportation (namely, trolleys) for several days with its twenty-six inches of snow. In those days, snow was shoveled into corner sewer drains, which eventually backed up. The storm caused seventy-seven deaths.

Subsequent blizzards attacked in 1996 with twenty inches of snow. That year, the city endured sixteen snowstorms with a total of eighty-nine inches of snow. Two feet of snow fell on the city on February 17, 2003. A two-day storm on February 11 and 12, 2006, produced twenty-six inches of snow.

Related to winter weather inconsistencies has been the freezing of our waterways. Back on January 19, 1852, the East River froze over, halting ferry traffic. (No bridge that year.) Hundreds of people who needed to cross from Brooklyn to New York had to walk across the ice floes. It happened again on February 9, 1856, and on January 23, 1867. But it wasn't just the East River; also freezing over were Gravesend Bay (February 5, 1902) and Sheepshead Bay (February 8, 1895).

Then, on March 1, 1925, Brooklyn felt a rumbling shock wave that was identified as a mild earthquake. Seismologists were not surprised, however, since a major fault runs under Brooklyn and Manhattan. Another followed on September 5, 1944. So far, we've not encountered the problems associated with California.

While weather forecasting has improved, saving lives of Brooklynites, surprises are always just around the corner, as September's tornado warned us. Who knows what's next? As Mark Twain supposedly remarked, "Everyone talks about the weather."

Brooklyn Under Water
September 15, 2011

The *Times* pointed out the problem last Tuesday. On Wednesday, Brooklyn searched for answers. Will Brooklyn be swamped by a one-hundred-year flood?

The answer is yes. Not only Brooklyn but also Queens and Staten Island. When? We don't know.

A panel held at Kingsborough Community College Wednesday evening voiced its opinion in the college's art gallery surrounded by pictures and maps from "Brooklyn's Waterfronts: Past, Present, Future." Sponsored by the Brooklyn Waterfront Research Center, the discussion drew an audience of over one hundred to hear the six panelists reveal their opinions on whether or not Brooklyn is at risk from climate change.

The panelists from the New York City College of Technology, Columbia University, New York's Department of City Planning as well as Kingsborough represented a range of academic fields: architecture, physics, biological sciences, English and history. While all agreed that a flooding danger exists, the solution to the problem was varied and inconclusive.

Suggestions included corrective measures used by other threatened communities: dikes, mounting buildings on pilings, building sea wall barriers. The solution revolved around costs; the problem, while inevitable, is not immediate. At least two of the panelists disagreed that a solution was possible. Klaus Jacob of Columbia University's Lamont-Dougherty Earth Observatory claimed that a sea barrier would not be effective because the height would be impractical and therefore an impossibility. Christina Colon of Kingsborough's biological sciences department claimed that nature's "diversity will save us" if we protect nature.

The problem, historically speaking, focuses on the global sea-level rise from 1870–2006, according to Reginald Blake of New York City Tech. Many of the homes bordering Jamaica Bay and in southern Brooklyn rest on filled-in sandy soil subject to erosion. City planners call it a "soft urban edge."

Betsy McCully of Kingsborough's English department addressed the natural history of New York City, citing the depletion of wetlands in Jamaica Bay for JFK Airport and Marine Park. On the positive side, she noted that the city and federal government are restoring these areas, allowing wetlands and grasslands to heal the earlier damage.

According to Michael Marrella, director of the city's waterfront with the department of planning, New York is addressing the potential situation with its open-space planning offered in PlaNYC for Vision 2020. These approaches include varied strategies for both one-hundred- and five-hundred-year plans through 1) changing the physical design of the city; 2) enhancing readiness; and 3) increasing the understanding of risks.

Many of these solutions seemed generalized and theoretical, but as Ilya Azaroff of City Tech stated at the opening of the conference, the "at risk" scenario must be examined before it's too late. In a wrap up, students in the audience were told that involvement and education are vital. On the more practical side, engineering with a nod to nature would help. The solution, everyone agreed, must be ethical, for the answers require hard decisions from politicians since governments do not have the resources to solve the immensity of the situation.

Kingsborough president Regina Peruggi opened the conference citing the *Times* article and directed the audience to find out what we need to know about the crisis. Richard Hanley, director of the Brooklyn Waterfront Research Center, stated that the situation is dire. (The arrival of Sandy on October 28, 2012, underlined the concern of the forum's participants.)

The conference was developed by Professor Libby Garland of Kingsborough's department of history, philosophy and political science and Professor Peter Malone of the art gallery, who curated the exhibit. The moderator was Michael Spear of Kingsborough.

The accompanying art exhibit consisted of photographs, art and maps depicting the Brooklyn waterfront and its ephemera.

Part IX

MEDIA

Brooklyn Newspapers to Touch
April 16, 2009

Newspapers now predict their own deaths—not only the major chains but also community papers and weeklies. Witness *The Brooklyn Paper*, Ed Weintrob's opus with his anti-Ratner campaign, which sold its soul to Rupert Murdoch, as did Brooklyn's *Courier* chain years ago. But newspapers always come and go. Now, though, they mostly go.

People say they need the feel of the printed page that they can't get from a computer or Kindle. Years ago, I bet people said, "I love the feel of leather reins in my hands. The steering wheel just doesn't do it for me."

Publishers are thrashing around today trying to make up for lost revenue with mergers, websites, live appearances and giveaways. Everybody's hurting. The *Eagle* certainly understands. This is its third resurrection.

Recently in this paper, Phoebe Neidl discovered a long-lost publication named *Brooklyn Life*, a "Home Weekly" that expired sometime in the 1920s, just about the time the country began encountering financial difficulties. According to Phoebe, the publication catered to Brooklyn society high life with articles about the good times. Its model may have been the *Ladies' Home Journal*. How about the *Brooklynite*? The Brooklyn Historical Society has an issue of that magazine on display in its library. It was published in the same time period, the 1920s. That may have been shaped after the *New Yorker*,

The Brooklyn Eagle building on Johnson Street. *Brooklyn Public Library, Brooklyn Collection/Kingsborough Historical Society.*

Dozier Hasty, publisher of the *Brooklyn Eagle*. *Photo by John Manbeck.*

which started publication in 1925. The *Brooklynite* contained fiction, poetry, art, reviews, sports and humor. Evidently, it was directed at the middle-aged crowd that lived around Brooklyn Heights. The editorial notes of a 1926 issue stated:

> *It is often the habit of the casual magazine reader, in classifying periodicals into types, to make comparisons. A new publication, therefore, must face this problem: it must overcome the stigma of imitation placed upon it when classified with that one or more magazines to which it may bear a comparison—however slight—in the eyes of the public.* [Note: The February 11 and 18, 2013 issues of the *New Yorker* paid tribute to the literary find.]

Ever read Brooklyn's the *Chat*? Not likely, unless you've been around seventy-five years or so, say between 1921–42. Or you might have traveled in your time machine to 1782, when Brooklyn's first newspaper was published: *Brooklyne Hall Super-Extra Gazette* (although it only lasted one issue). By the next century, the *Long Island Star* started publishing in 1809 but was dead by 1840. The *Brooklyn Evening Star* popped up the following year, publishing until 1863. Then the *East New York Real Estate Gazette* and *Williamsburg Democrat* emerged, followed by the *American Native Citizen and Brooklyn Evening Advertiser*.

By 1841, the original *Brooklyn Daily Eagle*, founded by Henry Cruse Murphy, started publishing, followed by the *Brooklyn Citizen* in 1854. These were the longest-lasting newspapers in Brooklyn. After the Civil War, the *Kings County Gazette, Brighton Gazette* and *Brooklyn Gazette* surfaced and then vanished. But they were accompanied by the *Brooklyn Daily Times* and the *Brooklyn Standard Union*, along with several special-interest publications: *Brooklyner Freie Presse*, a German-language newspaper; *NewYorkiin Uutiset*, a Finnish press; and the *Brooklyn Tablet*, a newspaper published by the Roman Catholic diocese. In the 1890s, Brooklyn proudly claimed over fourteen independent newspapers.

So they come and go. Our biggest loss occurred on March 16, 1955, when the *Brooklyn Eagle*, a national, full-coverage daily newspaper, went under. Since 1996, when Dozier Hasty assumed daily publication of the *Eagle* and combined it with the *Brooklyn Heights Press, Brooklyn Daily Bulletin* and Mike Armstrong's the *Phoenix*, the Brooklyn newspaper business has been an active world but primarily populated by community weeklies. But now times are more tenuous, even for the stately *New York Times*.

Long live the *Brooklyn Eagle*!

Radio Days in Brooklyn
August 13, 2009

"Don't touch that dial. Stay tuned for BROOKLYN!"

There never was a lead-in like that, but there should have been. When Lee De Forest sent out radio waves from the sands of Coney Island in the early twentieth century, Brooklyn knew it was "on the air."

Brooklyn caught the radio fever soon after the invention of the radio vacuum tube. In 1922, WGAC started broadcasting at 833 kilowatts, but it only lasted a year. As did WLBE, from 1926 to 1927. But others had more promise and excitement, like the "Brooklyn radio wars" fought in the Hotel St. George over air space and identity.

"Radioists," as the broadcasters were called during those Prohibition years, proliferated in Brooklyn, according to the NYC Radio History website. WBBC, the station operated by the Brooklyn Broadcasting Company in 1928, broadcast mostly foreign-language programming: Italian, German, Yiddish, Polish and "languages from Scandinavia." Competing with it was WLTH, founded in 1925 by the Flatbush Radio Laboratories at 1421 East Tenth Street. In 1928, it moved to the new Leverich Towers Hotel at 25 Clark Street in Brooklyn Heights as the "Voice of Brooklyn." With the Depression in 1929, the Leverich went into foreclosure and emerged as The Towers. The following year, the station moved into the *Brooklyn Eagle* building, proclaiming itself the "Voice of Brooklyn in the *Brooklyn Daily Eagle* building."

Primary programming consisted of foreign-language shows, but in 1933, the station paired with the Long Island Historical Society, today's Brooklyn Historical Society, to present a program called *Looking Back in Brooklyn*. In 1941, the cessation of the radio wars merged WARD, WBBC and WVFW into WBYN, which then morphed into WVNJ.

The aforementioned WVFW at 1430 kilowatts began in 1926 as WARS broadcasting from the Shelburne Hotel in Brighton Beach as the "Voice of the Atlantic." When the Shelburne was demolished a year later, the station moved to the Hotel St. George. In 1928, the call letters changed to WSGH, which programmed Seventh Day Adventist information. The next year, with the wars waging, the station moved from the hotel to 135 Eastern Parkway, switching to hybrid call letters WSGH-WSDA, selected for their owners. The station moved once more in 1930 to Brooklyn's Fox Theater, where it was known as WFOX. After three years, the latest name became WVFW, broadcasting from 49 Fourth Street as "the official voice of the Veterans of Foreign Wars." Programming consisted of veterans' news, as well as ethnic programming, mostly in Yiddish and Italian. In 1941, it joined the other Brooklyn broadcasters as the Unified Broadcasting Company and became WBYN.

Still in Brooklyn are other peripheral broadcasting operations, including WNYE, the board/department of education's official outlet with its antenna on the roof of Brooklyn Technical High School in Fort Greene. Another station, WEVD, operated primarily from Queens but in 1932 built its antenna in the Newtown Creek area. In 1936, WNYC, the city's municipal station, transmitted from Greenpoint.

The newest Brooklyn radio station began broadcasting on the FM band in 1978 from Kingsborough Community College in Manhattan Beach as WKRB-FM. As the faculty adviser, I had students start the station in 1972, naming it WKCC. As wired radio, it could not radiate and was heard only on campus. I encouraged the students to apply for an FM license because the transmitter was far away from interference. The call letters became WKRB for "Kingsborough Radio Brooklyn" because the original WKCC call letters address were taken by Kansas City. WKRB became the first new radio station in New York City in forty years.

In 2006, the station switched from 90.9 to 90.3 and became B91. As the "Rhythm of the City," the station is staffed by students from the college's communication program and has graduated several radio personalities.

I read that programs emanated from the Bossert Hotel in Brooklyn Heights as well. Whether it had its own station or just equipment, I haven't discovered. No matter—for a brief shining moment, Brooklyn was king of the airwaves.

Brooklyn's Movie Palaces
March 11, 2010

So you wanna see a movie?

Back in the old days (before television, DVDs, computers, cell phones and the Internet), movie theaters in Brooklyn were as plentiful as Starbucks are today. A half dozen alone clustered downtown near Fulton Street. They ran along most major thoroughfares (Flatbush Avenue, Kings Highway, Eighty-sixth Street, Utica and Church Avenues, Pitkin Avenue, etc.), and pocketed away on side streets were miniscule theaters commonly called the "itch" or the "dump." With new B movies released monthly, the film industry needed venues. Then there were the palaces—three thousand or more seats in theaters capable of presenting stage shows with orchestra pits and six-foot ushers. In fact, most of these large houses started as showplaces for plays and vaudeville but then converted to a "movie only" policy.

Today, most have disappeared—demolished to make way for a shopping mall or an office building, converted to multiplexes, transformed into houses of worship or left as piles of rubble. But last February 3, the *New York Times* announced that the only remaining palace in Brooklyn—Loew's Kings on Flatbush Avenue, vacant since 1977—got a reprieve. Logically, it will be converted to a theater for concerts, theatrical performances, community events and possibly an occasional film.

When it was built in 1929 on the site of a former barn for horse drawn trolley cars, Loew's Kings eventually competed with other smaller palaces on Church Avenue (RKO Kenmore), Kings Highway (Century's Kingsway) and the downtown behemoths Brooklyn Paramount, Brooklyn Strand, Brooklyn Fox, RKO Albee and Loew's Metropolitan, as well as others in Bay Ridge, Bensonhurst and East Flatbush.

The sixty-eight-thousand-square-foot interior of the Kings originally featured vaudeville acts and music from its pipe organ. A forty-five-minute color documentary on its history called *Memoirs of a Movie Palace* was released in 1980 by Blackwood Productions in hopes of luring potential buyers. That same year, newspapers listed the Kings as showing a film, *Almost Human*, although no information is available on the production.

Now, as a loner, it faces a $70 million renovation that will restore its original beauty, possibly even the basketball court in the basement, where ushers warmed up before going on duty. Neglected for over thirty years, it has been damaged by weather, birds and vandals. Owned by the city for back taxes, it is expected to reopen by 2015 with rehabilitation engineered by ACE Theatrical Group from Houston.

I have memories of the Loew's Kings as a neighborhood theater and of its luxurious lobby, where I saw several musicals as well as the films *Battleground* and *Psycho*. In my book *The Brooklyn Film* (McFarland & Company, 2003), Cezar Del Valle, a Brooklyn theater historian, wrote about Brooklyn's film history and its early movie theaters. He regards the latest proposed reincarnation with "guarded optimism," since $50 million is to come from the city's coffers.

With Kinetoscopes and small theaters in Coney Island and on Pitkin and Bushwick Avenues, Brooklyn started a love affair with movies in the early 1900s. Vitagraph Studios dominated suburban Midwood. Warner Brothers purchased the company in the mid-1920s, using Vitagraph's Flatlands warehouse to store material. Marcus Loew, later associated with Metro-Goldwyn-Mayer, opened his first theater, The Royal, in Brooklyn at Willoughby and Pearl Streets, according to Del Valle.

After 1913, popularity caused movie theaters to enlarge their seating space. Loew opened the Metropolitan on Fulton Street, with E.F. Albee competing down the street in 1925. William Fox not only built 200 theaters but also started the Fox film production company. Down on Flatbush Avenue, Paramount built its own palace. By 1927, 233 movie theaters operated in Brooklyn. And in 1929, the Kings, designed to resemble a faux palace at Versailles, opened as Brooklyn's third-largest movie house with 3,676 seats and Dolores Del Rio in the silent film *Evangeline*. (The star appeared at showings to say a few words, according to Del Valle.) But by the 1930s, the era of movie palaces had expired, giving way to smaller local houses with double bills and giveaway nights.

The end of the war introduced television into homes, forcing smaller theaters to close in the 1950s; larger ones were broken into multiplexes. But not the Kings. The bigger houses introduced stage shows, with rock-n-roll stars leading the pack, then succumbed to demolition teams or worse—porno houses. But others, such as "the Kings, continue to deteriorate behind boarded-up exteriors while awaiting an uncertain future," reported Del Valle in 2003.

Well, the future is now, and as of February, it looks rosy again for Loew's Kings.

Part X
LOST BROOKLYN

Remembering Joan Maynard
February 25, 2010

When I met Joan Maynard the first time, the Weeksville Heritage Center was only a dream, a figment of her rich imagination. We were both serving on the advisory board for the National Trust for Historic Preservation's New York convention. Then I found we had other commonalities: she served on the board of trustees for City University; I taught on a CUNY campus, Kingsborough. And we both knew Jim Hurley, then director of the Brooklyn Historical Society. Hurley was the force behind the rediscovery of the Hunterfly Road Houses, the heart of the Weeksville community.

Weeksville remains a linchpin in African American history because in 1838, eleven years after the abolition of slavery in New York, James Weeks purchased land near Brooklyn's Bedford Hills, later the Village of Bedford, today a part of Bedford-Stuyvesant. Houses soon rose on the plot, and another African American community, Carrsville, grew next to it in Crow Hill, a subdivision of Brooklyn's Eastern District.

By the 1850s, Weeksville—a seven-block area—claimed over five hundred residents as well as churches, a school ("Colored School No. 2"), a cemetery, an orphanage (Howard Orphan Asylum), an old-age home and a newspaper, the *Freedman's Torchlight*. With population growth and expansion

Joan Maynard receiving her award from Brooklyn Borough Historian John Manbeck. *Photo by Kathryn Kirk.*

of the City of Brooklyn after the opening of the Brooklyn Bridge (1883) and its consolidation into Greater New York in 1898, Weeksville was absorbed into Bedford-Stuyvesant and lost to history.

In 1968, Hurley, interested in discovering the location of Hunterfly Road, convinced pilot Joseph Haynes to fly over the area where four houses were discovered nested between Buffalo and Rochester Avenues. At that point, Joan Maynard, an art director for McGraw-Hill Publishing and a local activist, formed the Society for the Preservation of Weeksville & Bedford Stuyvesant History, with Hurley as its first president. In 1974, Maynard became its executive director. As the result of her driving force, the houses became New York City Landmarks in 1970 and the next year were placed on the National Register of Historic Places, from which she received its highest award.

Knowing Joan Maynard was to know a woman with a focused purpose. Every time she appeared in public and every time I met her, her primary purpose was to champion the Weeksville community and the African American cause, often as the "token black" in the organization. As chairman of the Mayor's Municipal Archives Advisory Board, I appointed her to serve as a director because of the quality of expertise she offered.

Her singular drive caused Weeksville to exist for many who contributed to its rehabilitation. Eventually, her perseverance convinced Senator Hillary Clinton to present the keynote speech in 2005 at the ceremony celebrating the restoration of the Weeksville houses.

Joan Maynard received many deserving awards for her service, including one from the Landmarks Conservancy and a posthumous Lifetime Achievement Award from Brooklyn District Attorney Charles Hynes. She died in 2006, leaving a living legacy for the preservation of black history in historic Weeksville.

Everett Ortner, Brownstone Revival Leader
May 31, 2012

Everett Ortner, the Brooklyn preservationist who with his wife, Evelyn, helped reinvent Park Slope, died May 22 of a heart attack and complications from a fall on May 3, according to a spokesperson. He was ninety-two and died in New York Methodist Hospital.

After co-founding the Brownstone Revival Committee of New York in 1968, Ortner worked in the 1970s with the Brooklyn Union Gas Company (now National Grid) to develop the Cinderella Projects that promoted Brooklyn's historic communities. Cinderella grants installed gas lamps, assisted in renovations (some based on the suggestions of Evelyn Ortner) and underwrote a series of Brownstone Fairs and films, including *The Brownstones of Berkeley Place* and *The Brownstones of Brooklyn*. When I interviewed Everett Ortner in 2010, he observed, "Brownstones were acceptable but certainly not fashionable" in the mid-1960s. The Ortners were once offered two houses on Sixth Avenue for $25,000. At the time, malaise and abandonment swept Park Slope from Fifth Avenue to Prospect Park. Realtors approached glorious brownstones and sandstones primarily to reconfigure them into rooming houses or to demolish them. In 1963, the Ortners purchased the 1886 Elsie Hinkins home at 272 Berkeley Place for $32,000, which remained original and pristine throughout their lifetime. Within the past five years, Ortner was offered over $4 million for his home.

Ortner, born in Lowell, Massachusetts, into a middle-class household, moved to Brooklyn, where his father sold medical supplies. As a graduate from the University of Arkansas, a first-class school with "reasonable rates," as he described it, Ortner earned a degree in humanities and learned skill as a writer. But that was 1939, when jobs were scarce and a war was just around the corner.

He enlisted and fought in France and Germany, emerging from World War II as a lieutenant, having spent seven months as a German prisoner of war. After his release, Ortner returned to New York, where he found that the publishing field had opened and editors were willingly hiring returning GIs. He eventually landed on the editorial staff of *Popular Science* magazine, launching a career that allowed him to travel, write stories, take photographs and have a wonderful life between 1953 and 1985, when he retired as editor in chief.

The Ortners had lived in Brooklyn Heights in the 1960s, when brownstones sold for $35,000 and up. Park Slope residences went from zero and up. From the time they moved into Park Slope, they began to promote the livability of the neighborhood.

Contacting new residents in 1965 (Ortner recalled that there were only forty of them), the Ortners asked them to promote Park Slope by encouraging friends to invest in their new neighborhood. None of the newcomers ever complained. Houses they bought then for $20,000 are now valued in the millions.

In 1972, the brownstone revival moved one step further. Funded by Brooklyn Union, Everett Ortner founded a "Back to the City" movement, a national drive to promote urban revival. A weekend program drew 250 representatives to New York City from eighty-one American cities, all looking for programs to bring new life to dying American cities. Both Ortners went international in 1998 and founded an exchange program for French and American volunteers to work on preservation programs. In 2010, an interview with Everett Ortner was recorded by Brooklyn College for its archive library.

As Everett Ortner said, brownstone and sandstone buildings are not distinctive to Brooklyn, but they make Brooklyn distinctive. When no one cares, a city dies. Everett and Evelyn Ortner made sure it didn't happen in Brooklyn.

Evelyn Ortner died in 2006. The Ortners had no children but have relatives in Cleveland, Ohio; Westchester, New York; and Delray Beach, Florida. A private memorial service for Everett will be held at Green-Wood Cemetery at a later date.

Matt Kennedy, ninety-seven, talking to a reporter in 2002. *Photo by John Manbeck.*

Matt Kennedy, Centurion
May 4, 2006

Matt Kennedy, a Coney Island legend—a centurion at age 101—died five days after St. Patrick's Day. On that day, he had visited Borough Hall for an Irish breakfast hosted by Borough President Marty Markowitz. As a senior citizen, Kennedy remained incredibly active.

I first met Matt back in the 1970s, when he was president of the Coney Island Chamber of Commerce. The office was located on the second floor of a building on Surf Avenue and Fifteenth Street over what had been an attraction for baby animals, just south of Gargiulo's Restaurant. I accompanied Gail Smollon and John Rossi, then supervising the Kingsborough Historical Society, who had contacted him. He gave them historic Coney Island artifacts from his collection for the society. Several months later, the building burned to the ground, destroying shelves full of Coney Island history and nostalgia.

Back when Matt was only eighty-six, David Isay from National Public Radio (NPR) had interviewed him. Isay told of how Kennedy answered the phone: "Yes, of course Coney Island still exists. Yes, it's bigger and better than ever." In Matt's mind, the beach never held fewer than one million beachgoers. He ran the chamber from 1968 until he retired in 1990 for "health reasons" at ninety. Kennedy had been born in a house next to Coney Island Creek when it ran from Gravesend Bay into Sheepshead Bay. In his lifetime, he crossed paths with famous and infamous, from Teddy Roosevelt to gangster Frankie Uale, according to *New York Times* writer Douglas Martin.

Kennedy's grandfather had been a lighthouse keeper at Norton's Point (now Sea Gate), and his father had been a young police lieutenant when Dreamland burned in 1911, noted Charles Denson, author of *Coney Island Lost and Found.* In between, Matt defended Coney Island's rowdy present and pressured politicians for a baseball team. Mayor Rudy Giuliani finally granted his wish with the Cyclones.

At his death, Kennedy claimed twenty-five great-grandchildren and five great-great-grandchildren. His granddaughter Maureen Gillespie cared for him. According to Dick Zigun of Coney Island USA, he lunched on liverwurst sandwiches made with Wonder Bread.

After losing contact with Matt for about fifteen years, I met him once more at the seventy-fifth birthday celebration of the Cyclone roller coaster in 2002. Thinking that a man in his late nineties had every right to be forgetful, I reintroduced myself. He studied me, wagged his cigar and asked, "Do you still live on East Thirty-second Street?" So much for senility.

His granddaughter told me he still liked to cook and often invited friends in for a meal. However, his failing eyesight sometimes created unusual flavors for his meals. In his long lifetime, he would not be defeated by Coney Island, by recipes or by life's peccadilloes.

Long live Matt Kennedy!

Olga Bloom, the Sound of Bargemusic
January 12, 2012

The saddest news from 2011 was the Thanksgiving Day death of Olga Bloom, the inspired voice behind Brooklyn's Bargemusic. Her vision to convert a nineteenth-century coffee barge into a floating concert hall remains a tribute to her memory. I'll always remember attending a New Year's Eve chamber concert in 1999 as the millennium closed. The cold outside was warded off by the musical warmth and camaraderie inside. Even the wake of passing boats contributed to the musical tempos on board for both musicians and the audience. Often, when Olga was in good health, the audience encouraged her to play a selection on her violin or viola. The benches that she had installed twenty-five years ago created an ambiance cherished by all.

Bargemusic initially provided a haven for struggling musicians but then developed into a Brooklyn cultural icon respected throughout New York City. It now offers 220 concerts a year—four days a week, fifty-two weeks a year—and acts as a venue for special rentals and events. The annual budget for Bargemusic exceeds $1 million today, but it offers free concerts every month. Its musical menu also features jazz programming in a concert setting.

Bloom, born Olga Bayrack in Boston, studied to become a professional violinist and violist, playing both for conductor Leopold Stokowski and in pits for Broadway shows. Her first husband, also a violinist, died in World War II. Her second husband, Tobias Bloom, played violin as well, for the NBC Symphony Orchestra under Arturo Toscanini, back when radio stations employed full-time musicians. When Tobias died in the 1970s, Olga Bloom embarked on a search for a barge that was acoustically sound. After several disappointments, she found success. It was the one-hundred-foot *EL 375* steel barge, formerly property of the Erie Lackawanna Railroad, for which she paid $10,000. Refurbishing it was the hard part, but with contributions of material and labor, Olga painted it white and refashioned the working industrial barge into a 140-seat concert hall.

Moored next to the historic Fulton Ferry Landing, Bargemusic floats in the epicenter of Brooklyn's waterfront attractions, with the Brooklyn Bridge above and River Café and Dumbo steps from its pilings. In recent years, the Brooklyn Ice Cream Factory moved into the former Maritime Museum (once a firehouse), the popular Brooklyn Bridge Park stretches out on the shore and now Jane's Carousel provides entertainment for the younger set. Year-round, the landing remains a port for the East River Ferry and the Water Taxi.

In 2005, Olga relinquished operation of Bargemusic to violinist Mark Peskanov, who was named president and artistic director. Still, there is music in the air of the Brooklyn waterfront because Olga Bloom had the vision and persistence, assuring us that Bach would remain an integral part of our lives after she was gone.

Plans are in preparation for a memorial concert in tribute to Bargemusic's ninety-two-year-old matriarch, Olga Bloom.

Part XI

BROOKLYN CRIME

Pirates of Sheepshead Bay
March 10, 2011

The pirates of the Caribbean, they were not. Not a Johnny Depp or Gregory Rush character among them. Not even like the Barbary pirates that Thomas Jefferson sent our marines to fight. If the government didn't pay a ransom for captured ships, the Berbers got nasty. They came from places like Tripoli, Tunisia and Algiers, all names in the current news. And they did war on Spain, France and Italy, sacking coastal towns for slaves. Our Brooklyn pirates were more like the killer pirates from Somalia. Now that's scary. As with most pirates, they transformed from privateers—civilians who attacked enemy ships with the unofficial blessing of the government—who found civilian life boring after a war was over and turned into mercenaries.

The time we're talking about is the early nineteenth century—the winter of 1830. At the time, Coney Island, a grazing place in the Town of Gravesend, was sparsely settled, with a small hotel and a few shacks on the beach. In Sheepshead Bay, the remains of an old Indian village, Sam Leonard had opened a bar for the few local farmers. A brig, a two-masted oceangoing ship, the *Vineyard*, had set sail from New Orleans to Philadelphia with bales of cotton, casks of molasses and a cache of gold destined for the Stephen Girard bank. The sum was $54,000 in coin.

The *Vineyard* was under the command of Captain William Thornby. Among the crew was a sailor who signed on as Charles Gibbs; his real name was James Jeffers. Though only thirty-three, by that time he admitted to killing (mostly by decapitation) and maiming over four hundred victims. He had left his Rhode Island home in 1816 at seventeen to become a privateer but soon mutinied and began roaming the Caribbean as a pirate. His exploits included fighting with Barbary Corsairs before signing on with Captain Thornby as a seaman. Among other members of the *Vineyard* crew were Thomas Wansley, the black cook and steward; Robert Dawes, the cabin boy; James Talbot; Aaron Church; Henry Atwell; and John Brownrigg—all seamen. (Blacks became seamen because they felt they were treated more fairly at sea.)

On the night of November 23, the mutineers struck. They attacked both the captain and the first mate William Roberts, throwing them overboard. Then Gibbs ordered the brig to sail north for Long Island, where they dropped anchor in Jamaica Bay between the Rockaways and Pelican Island. They divided the treasure into bags containing $5,000 each, loaded them into the two lifeboats, set fire to the ship and escaped for shore at dawn. Caught in surf, they threw some of the money overboard. The other yawl capsized, and the three men—Church, Talbot and Atwell—drowned with $23,000 lost. Gibbs/Jeffers and his boat mates—Wansley, Brownrigg and Dawes—landed on Barren Island (today's Floyd Bennett Field and Gateway National Recreation Area), where they buried the money in the sand. There they met William Johnson, who offered them shelter in Dooley's Inn. While the others slept, Brownrigg told Johnson the complete story. As soon as he could, Johnson went to find the buried treasure, but he only secured part of the loot.

The next day, the sailors moved on to Sam Leonard's bar in Sheepshead Bay for food and drink and transit to Manhattan. Flushed, the men quarreled, and Brownrigg confessed again. Gibbs and Dawes were seized and bound by the innkeeper. The portly Wansley escaped but was soon captured in the woods. Brownrigg and Dawes turned state's evidence, sending Gibbs and Wansley to Bridewell Prison, where they were convicted of murder, moved to Bellevue Prison and hanged on Ellis Island on April 22, 1831. Before his execution, Gibbs confessed to a series of (possibly exaggerated) crimes. The pirates of Sheepshead Bay were the last pirates executed in New York.

Of the fortune, $16,000 was lost to the tides but partially recovered in 1842 by William Johnson and other fortune seekers. At least in Sheepshead Bay, piracy didn't pay.

Ward Politics
October 30, 2008

Today, our elections remain relatively tepid, aside from glitches in voting machines. Not so in the nineteenth century, when ward politics ruled local government. Back then, "wards" in the cities of New York and Brooklyn were the smallest unit of political districts created for the purposes of elections. The term came from British and Scottish election districts and has been transformed into today's election districts (ED). Other American communities call them townships, boroughs or parishes, for the same purpose.

Tammany Hall, founded in 1788 as the Society of St. Tammany, became the most colorful synonym of corrupt ward politics. But the ward system dated back to 1686, when British governor Thomas Dongan divided Manhattan into six wards with the initial charter for New York. They were named North, East, South, West, Dock and Out, according to the *Encyclopedia of New York City*. In 1731, a seventh ward was added, named Montgomerie after Governor John Montgomerie. The common council, today's city council, replaced the names with numbers in 1791.

As the city grew, so too did the number of wards, until Manhattan had increased to twenty-two wards. The wards elected aldermen (today's council members) and assistant aldermen to the common council. The aldermen appointed tax assessors, tax collectors and constables, so by 1800, the possibilities for corruption in the more powerful wards increased, as the "ward bosses" or district leaders controlled the police, fire, sanitation and judicial services. In the nineteenth century, fifteen of New York's twenty-two wards were south of Fourteenth Street, where the city's greatest wealth was concentrated.

The ward system reeked of inequality. "American" wards, the ninth and fifteenth, had low immigrant populations, while in the fourth and sixth wards, 70 percent of residents were immigrants. African Americans lived in the fifth, sixth and eighth wards. The most heavily populated was the seventeenth ward.

New city charters in 1853 and 1857 replaced "wards" with "districts" for city and state elections, but the change was semantic, so the same corruption prevailed. The City of Brooklyn operated under a similar system when the government created nine wards in 1837. The first ward was Brooklyn Heights, the seat of its municipal government. In Brooklyn, aldermen served two-year terms. By 1898, the date of Brooklyn's consolidation with New

York, Brooklyn had thirty-two wards. Manhattan had added two more wards in 1873 when New York annexed land in lower Westchester for the Bronx.

Tammany, initially founded by Aaron Burr and Martin Van Buren in 1789, adapted the role as provider of social services. It saw its responsibility as protector of friendless immigrants, helping them toward citizenship. In exchange, the organization asked for votes.

Named after a Delaware Indian chief, Tamanend, and originally composed of craftsmen, the Tammany organization catered to the needs of immigrants, who were mostly Irish. Its 1868 headquarters at Third Avenue and Fourteenth Street was known as the wigwam, while its officers were "sachems" and members "braves." As Tammany began to gain political power and influence over votes, it supported candidates such as Mayor Fernando Wood, the first Tammany-backed mayor in 1854, who created a police force to rival the one appointed by Albany. But largely, Tammany bosses who were not elected controlled politics by securing votes and by providing services for immigrants. As the Irish dominated Tammany's membership, Italians, blacks and other minorities were ignored.

Several Tammany bosses emerged as leaders who affected state and national politics. The most infamous, William Tweed, who is buried in Brooklyn's Green-Wood Cemetery, started as a bookkeeper and chair maker. His creation of the John J. Reilly Volunteer Fire Company earned him a seat in Tammany in 1849. By 1852, he was elected to the U.S. House of Representatives, was "appointed" as a lawyer and became the grand sachem of Tammany in 1863.

While his personal wealth increased significantly during his tenure, Tweed also founded the Manhattan Eye and Ear Hospital, sat on the board of the Brooklyn Bridge Corporation, widened Broadway and supported the creation of Central Park and the Metropolitan Museum of Art. For his fraud, Tweed was arrested, but he still won a seat as a state senator in spite of being indicted. Finally, as a result of articles in the *New York Times* and caricatures drawn by Brooklyn artist Thomas Nast, Tweed was sentenced to twelve years in Ludlow Prison in 1873. The investigations had been initiated by reformer Samuel Tilden, the state Democratic leader. Tammany expelled Tweed for his misdeeds.

In 1875, Tweed escaped to New Jersey but was recaptured and faced a civil trial. Again Tweed escaped, this time to Coney Island and then to Florida, Cuba and Spain, where he was finally arrested when a customs agent recognized him from Nast's cartoon. In 1877, he returned to New York to complete his sentence.

Arrest of Gravesend/Coney Island ward boss John Y. McKane. *Brooklyn College Library Archives.*

Following Tweed, John Kelly rose to power in 1872, while Richard Croker, born in Dublin and a boxer, started as a member of the "Fourth Avenue Tunnel Gang" and was elected as alderman and finally Tammany leader in 1886. In 1894, Albany investigated New York police corruption, which led to the election of former Brooklyn mayor Seth Low. Tammany politics survived into the mid-twentieth century, with Carmine DeSapio of Greenwich Village possibly the last practitioner.

Among notable Tammany members were Civil War general, congressman and murderer Dan Sickles and the often-quoted George Washington Plunkitt, a state senator. Plunkitt was a loyal machine member who practiced "honest graft." "I seen my opportunities, and I took 'em," he admitted in defense of his actions. Some activities never change.

Brooklyn, of course, was not exempt from this chicanery. The most visible Brooklyn boss was Hugh McLaughlin, but the kingdom by the sea lorded over by John Y. McKane certainly qualified as redolent of Tammany's corruption. Known as "the autocrat of Gravesend" and "the Grand Poo-Bah of Coney Island," he controlled Coney Island politics from 1881 until he retired to Sing Sing Penitentiary in 1894.

Brooklyn's Crime Families
May 28, 2009

A friend of mine, Professor Bob Blaisdell from Kingsborough Community College, once asked me, "What do you know about crime in Brooklyn?" I replied that I knew about Brooklyn grime but little about crime. "Do we have crime in Brooklyn?"

"Not now," he informed me, "but years ago, Brooklyn was renowned for its crime families. As a former Brooklyn Borough Historian, will you come to talk to my class about Brooklyn crime? My Dostoyevsky class discovered crime in Russia, and that's just down the street in Brighton Beach."

And sure enough, I consulted my well-worn "Curmudgeon" book and found that Oscar Wilde once said, "Americans are certainly great hero-worshipers and always take their heroes from the criminal classes." So why not Brooklynites?

I was shocked to read that Murder Inc started in Brooklyn—the Brownsville Boys, they called themselves. But I was relieved that they weren't the Italian stereotypes that you see in the movies. They were fine upstanding Brooklyn Jewish boys from good families. They also called themselves the Brooklyn Combination.

Many had nicknames because they were shy about revealing their true identities. Some of these monikers you may have heard: Bugsy, Three-Fingered Brown, The Mad Hatter, Harry the Horse, Joe the Baker, The Jerk, The Brain, Society Max, Dandy Jack, Nathan Detroit, Rusty Charlie. You probably heard them in the musical *Guys and Dolls*. Damon Runyon, who wrote the stories the play was based on, earned his living as a scribe, or newspaper reporter. He would hang out in Times Square, where some of these high rollers schmoozed, and tuned in to their jargon about sports (racing) and other activities too sensitive to mention.

We're talking history now—1920s, '30s and '40s. And y'know, boys will be boys. They would hang out, just like kids still do. Their hangout was Midnight Rose's, a candy store at Saratoga and Livonia Avenues, and drink egg creams and munch on pretzels. What, you never heard of an egg cream? Well, at Midnight Rose's, they'd get the call—never at home on Van Siclen Avenue or on Vermont. And then they'd take a little trip, see? They wouldn't be seen with Mafia or Cosa Nostra members. They had their own little jokes—they called themselves the Kosher Nostra.

Their names were strictly "old neighborhood": Weiss, Cohen, Schultz, Lansky, Shapiro, Rubin, Rosenkrantz, Schecter. And they worked hard at their jobs. They were businessmen. The bosses were Louis Buchalter and Benjamin Siegel, also known as "Bugsy," but not to be confused with Buggsy Goldstein. They signed contracts. Operating from their Brooklyn base, they ran a national outfit and established a fee structure—$1,000 to $5,000 a commission to their "salesmen" above their weekly retainer. And this was during the Depression. Their jobs required them to use special tools such as knives, ice picks, ropes and even butcher cleavers. They seldom used guns, unless they were big, noisy ones called Tommy guns, after Thompson machine guns.

Like any profitable business, they diversified and had holding companies in other fields: liquor (when it was profitable, during Prohibition), drugs, prostitution, racketeering, gambling. But it was all in the family. And they were like family, but the one thing that riled them was gossip. They didn't like being talked about, particularly to the police. But that's the way kids are, y'know?

They also found that they were not the only kids on the block, y' know what I mean? Around the corner, so to speak, there was the Ocean Hill Hooligans, the Italian faction. And as their mothers told them, play nice. So they began to work with Harry Maione, the leader, in a way. He had a few friends, such as Joe Adonis, Tommy Lucchese and Albert "The Mad Hatter" Anastasia, some of whom jockeyed for the role of lead honcho over the years.

Other golden hits happened all over town. One night in 1931, Joe "The Boss" Masseria dined with "Lucky" Luciano at Nuova Villa Tammari at 2715 West Fifteenth Street in Coney Island. Lucky excused himself to see a man about a horse, as they say. Just then, four customers walked in: Joey Adonis, Vito Genovese, Albert Anastasia and Bugsy Siegel. Joe was no longer "The Boss." Later, Anastasia bit the sawdust in a barber chair at the Park Sheraton across from Carnegie Hall. Y' hafta know how to play the game.

Another Brooklyn boy, Alphonse Capone, lived at 38 Garfield Place as a child in 1937. He worked at the Harvard Inn, a Coney Island dance hall (where he became "Scarface"), married Brooklynite Mae Coughlin and then moved to Chicago, where he hit the big time.

Frankie Yale (aka Uale), another Brooklyn alumni, had several professions. He was an undertaker at 6604 Fourteenth Avenue in Bay Ridge, owned the Yale Cigar Factory at 6309 New Utrecht Avenue in Bensonhurst and was gunned down at 923 Forty-fourth Street in Borough Park. You might say he lived and died in Brooklyn.

Meanwhile, in 1979 over in Bushwick, a businessman (heroin, racketeering) named Carmine Galente was enjoying his lunch at Joe &

Police confiscate a pile of guns at a crime scene, 1947. *Brooklyn Public Library, Brooklyn Collection.*

Mary's Luncheonette at 205 Knickerbocker Avenue until three men wearing ski masks and carrying shotguns approached him.

To the west in Red Hook, a hood named "Crazy Joe" Gallo lived peacefully in a residential neighborhood. He descended from criminal elements, as his father and brothers were in the same racket. One of his hit men, accused of the Anastasia execution, was killed in Sheepshead Bay by rival gang leader Joseph Profacia. "Crazy Joe" himself was executed in 1972 while dining in Little Italy's Umberto's Clam House. Gallo is buried in Brooklyn's Green-Wood Cemetery.

But not all of Brooklyn's crime stories are bloody. Ever hear of Willie "The Actor" Sutton? He robbed banks but disliked hurting people. He lived on Dean Street in Park Slope and later on High Street in Dumbo. His twenty bank robberies netted him over $2 million.

Then, back on August 31, 1931, the *New York Times* ran a story back on page 24 (crime stories were unseemly back then) headlined "Gang Firing Squad Surrenders in Raid." In a copycat crime suggested by Chicago's St.

Valentine's Day Massacre, ex-marine Barney Wolfson, twenty-two, was arrested in Bushwick with three of his Brooklyn friends. Charged with the execution murders of three young men against a lumberyard wall, Wolfson, a marksman in the war, had a grudge against only one. The others had simply shown up at the wrong place, wrong time. After his prison sentence, Wolfson retired to the sunshine of Florida.

Another Florida retiree was Cecilia Cooney, known in the press as "The Bobbed-Haired Bandit." In 1924, bobbed hair was the latest fashion. With the help of her husband, Ed, nineteen-year-old Cecilia robbed a string of Brooklyn and New York grocery stores. She always wore a fur coat and brandished a "baby automatic," thereby becoming a mysterious but fashionable celebrity.

By the 1930s, the random bodies turning up in fields and floating in the Gowanus embarrassed the law enforcers. A state prosecutor appeared on the scene—a dapper, serious man with a serious mustache named Thomas Dewey. In New York, another serious district attorney, William O'Dwyer, also directed his attention to the "mob." Both seemed to have ambition for higher office. By the 1940s, most of the crime was cleaned up, on the surface.

In Brooklyn, a particularly garrulous stool pigeon named Abe Reles was helpful. He used the nickname "Kid Twist," a name that had been used in the nineteenth century by a Coney Island tough who had some similar nasty habits. As a hit man, Reles's specialty was the rope, a sharp knife and an ice pick. In the movies, he was played by Peter Falk. The movie's title was *Murder Inc.*

After his testimony, the prosecutors felt that they should keep Reles safe in a remote location: Coney Island, where the Half Moon Hotel was empty in winter. There he had not a suite but two top floors protected by a squadron of police. Mysteriously, he tried to escape one November night in 1941, but shortsightedly he short-sheeted himself. When he reached the end of the sheets he was climbing down, he fell the other four floors to his death. The subsequent trial used the sheets as evidence. After the trial, several high-ranking police retired far away.

The verdict? Death by defenestration. Reporters speculated that he knew too much about how the city really operated.

Prohibition in Brooklyn
October 20, 2011

With the recent telecast of Ken Burns's *Prohibition* on PBS, I thought it would be fun to read how it was reported in the *Brooklyn Daily Eagle* of yore. It's exciting to look through those pages. Did you know the *Eagle* had its own radio station—WAHG—or that in 1913 the borough president appointed his own cabinet? Well, here's what I found about Prohibition in the *Brooklyn Eagle*.

As Burns's documentary explains, the legal fight against alcohol as a social scourge began before the Civil War, but it was not until the Anti-Saloon League teamed with the Women's Temperance Christian Union (WCTU) that the Eighteenth Amendment became a reality, taking effect in 1920. As Pete Hamill observed, it was the only amendment that stated what Americans could not do: manufacture, sell or transport any alcoholic beverages.

With its sixty-five miles of waterfront, Brooklyn became a natural for rumrunners, boats that delivered "hooch" to the false rear of garages in Brighton Beach and elsewhere. By 1924, the *Eagle* began to print regular coverage on the dangers of illegal drinks and raids on speakeasies. "Brooklyn is Overrun with Bootleggers and Speakeasies" a headline ran, followed by a half-page cartoon in which Death plays a fiddle while dangerous bottles of gin, whiskey and rum dance around. "POISON HOOTCH FLOODING NEW YORK" screamed the banner.

Fiorello LaGuardia, then a congressman, declared that Prohibition was a "noble experiment" but was unenforceable and discriminatory to immigrants. Stories appeared of raids on homes in which cellars contained bottles of wine and beer. Many of the residents had Italian names.

As speakeasies opened across the city, authorities tallied over thirty-two thousand, twice the number of legitimate saloons before Prohibition. Organized crime recognized an opportunity. Local Brooklyn criminals Al Capone and Joey Yale became involved, eventually achieving nationwide infamy. Stories of murder and gang wars associated with racketeer Charles "Lucky" Luciano and "Legs" Diamond also began appearing in print.

Aside from the professional criminals, a story exposed a "Huge Rum Ring" financed by Brooklyn banks and law firms. A week later, six Brooklyn doctors allied with a pharmacist prescribed rum for ailments, then a "Booze Party" on Wall Street was hosted by the president of the Lehigh Valley Railroad. Twenty-six Brooklyn physicians were fined for selling "medicinal whisky." The Women's National Committee for Law Enforcement testified for Brooklyn Representative Emanuel Celler that "Rum Buyers" were as guilty as the distillers.

By 1931, the *Eagle* reported on gang shootings and murders in Gravesend. The party was turning nasty. Al Capone, "a Brooklyn boy," was surprised to be accused of income tax evasion in 1931. Then the expenditures for the Association Against the Prohibition Amendment were subpoenaed. In 1933, the tide against the amendment was flowing even though Club Henrei, in Flatbush at 630 Ocean Avenue and Albemarle Road, was raided by Prohibition officials. A month later, the *Eagle*'s banner head read, "HOUSE VOTES REPEAL."

Afterward, Albany held a hearing on beer, and in April 1933, the paper reported, "Thousands Wait for City Beer Permits." Free beer was offered at Coney Island. They called it "Brew Year's Eve." In November, repeal was voted by the states, and President Roosevelt signed the bill. To clean up, the unlicensed speakeasies were raided and closed.

And so a shadowy era in our nation's history passed—one that is more embarrassing than praiseworthy. But the *Brooklyn Eagle* reported the facts, as a good national daily would do.

Part XII

BROOKLYN GOES TO WAR

Fate of Our Fathers
July 1 and 8, 2010

History plays many tricks on us. Take the Fourth of July, for instance. Is it the celebration of the signing of the Declaration of Independence? Think again.

July 2 began the signatory process, according to *Signing Their Lives Away*, by Denise Kiernan and Joseph D'Agnese (Quirk Books). Forget about that room in Philadelphia and all the signers impatiently waiting in line to inscribe the document with "the Liberty Bell tolling for each signer." Forget about it!

With the first unofficial vote on July 1, nine colonies (out of thirteen) supported breaking with England. South Carolina and Pennsylvania voted "No." Delaware deadlocked, while New York abstained. In the official vote on July 2, twelve voted in favor. New York again abstained. Only two signed on the day of the official vote: John Hancock and his secretary, Charles Thomson, now considered the fifty-seventh signer.

Over the next two days, the wording was polished. July 4 came and went, and still only two names had been signed. The Declaration was printed by John Dunlap without signatures, and two hundred copies with the date of July 4, 1776, were distributed throughout the former colonies. But with transportation being what it was in the eighteenth century, most of the signers did not affix their names to the document until August 2. Congress

Declaration of Independence. *Author's collection.*

aided and abetted this act by backdating relevant documents to show that all fifty-six men had already signed the record. However, the fifty-six men who voted for independence were not the same who signed the Declaration on August 2. A war was being fought, so some of the originals were fighting, traveling, in other positions or had been replaced as delegates. The final signature wasn't recorded until 1781.

Old Stone House. *Photo by John Gallagher.*

In Brooklyn, the streets of Williamsburg are named after the signers, all of whom had jeopardized their lives since British troops occupied the colonies for sixteen years after the signing of the Declaration. So what happened to them, particularly those representing New York and, more specifically, the three known in Brooklyn?

Charles Carroll, the only Roman Catholic to sign, is remembered in the names Carroll Street and Carroll Gardens, although he never set foot in Kings County. Why? Carroll represented Maryland, and that fact alone should hint at why Brooklynites honor him. Think Battle of Brooklyn. The Marylanders fought (and lost) and suffered the greatest number of casualties in that attack on the Old Stone House. But that skirmish allowed George Washington to escape to Manhattan, thereby preserving our independence.

Carroll, a wealthy planter, was the last signer to die. He died the richest man in America in 1832. As a Catholic in the Anglican British colonies, Carroll endured prejudice. Catholics couldn't vote, hold public office, teach or practice law in England or the colonies. But Carroll was a lawyer, educated in France and at a law school in England. He moved to Annapolis and raised a family. Not able to practice law, he turned to writing broadsides against taxes and the government.

From there, Carroll attended revolutionary conventions and went to Philadelphia as an unofficial member of the Maryland delegation. As a result of Carroll's charm and influence, the Maryland delegation voted for independence. While he was not in Philadelphia on July 2, he was chosen as representative on July 4. He arrived in Philadelphia on July 18 in time to sign the final document.

A strong supporter of General Washington, Carroll visited him in Valley Forge and provided troops for General William Alexander in the Battle of Brooklyn. Later, he served as one of Maryland's first U.S. senators. In his last forty years, he managed his land—more than seventy thousand acres—and his hundreds of slaves, although he freed many of them before his death and in 1789 introduced a bill for the gradual abolition of slavery. Living to be ninety-five, he outlived both Jefferson and Adams.

The other name misremembered in Brooklyn is that of Thomas McKean, whose signature looked like "Tho. M. Keap," thereby rendering Brooklyn's Keap Street. McKean was Delaware's governor while serving as the chief justice of Pennsylvania. He also was the last man to sign the Declaration in 1781, five years after everyone else.

Initially a lawyer who practiced in both Delaware and New Jersey, McKean was eventually sent to Congress to serve eight years as representative of Delaware (even though he lived in Philadelphia.) McKean's fame increased when he sent a messenger to bring in a sickly Caesar Rodney to vote for independence for Delaware. By the end of July, McKean led a Pennsylvania militia to aid Washington in his defense of New York.

With British troops hunting him, he ran with his wife and eleven children. But in 1781, McKean served as president of Congress, holding the title of President of the United States in Congress Assembled before the first general election of Washington. By 1799, he had served three terms as governor of Pennsylvania, although those years were so contentious that his critics tried to have him impeached. He died wealthy in 1817 and was buried in Philadelphia.

In his last years, McKean claimed that no one had signed the Declaration on July 4, although this was disputed by Jefferson at the age of seventy-six. In truth, at least seven of the signers were not elected to Congress until after July 4, 1776.

Other New York signers of the Declaration were mostly rich landowners from upstate: Philip Livingston, William Floyd, Francis Lewis and Lewis Morris. Livingston was the only Brooklynite.

Livingston owned about 160,000 acres on the Hudson, but his home, which Washington used as his headquarters, was in Brooklyn. His family fled to the new New York capital at Kingston, so the British seized and subsequently burned his homes. Although Livingston suffered financially after the loss, his family eventually built forty mansions along the banks of the Hudson. Because British troops occupied Philadelphia, Congress met in York, Pennsylvania, where Livingston died of heart failure in 1778.

Floyd, a wealthy land speculator, lived on Long Island near Fire Island. Involved in the local militia, he drifted into politics and the First Continental Congress. When the New York colony accepted the Declaration, Floyd was first to sign it on July 9. His family escaped the British occupation by crossing Long Island Sound to Connecticut. Returning home after the peace treaty, he found his home ruined but salvageable. He then moved to a farm in upstate New York, where he died at eighty-six.

Lewis, a merchant who signed the Declaration at sixty-three, lost the most out of the New York signers. Captured in the French and Indian War, he later joined patriot groups and signed the Declaration on August 2. British soldiers attacked and destroyed his Long Island home and imprisoned his wife. After being traded by Washington for two Tory wives, she was released but forced to remain in New York City. She died just two years later. Lewis moved in with his sons and died at ninety.

Morris, a planter who lived in Morrisania (now in the Bronx), originally owned several thousand acres north of New York City. When the British taxed New Yorkers for billeting soldiers, Morris objected. Sent as a representative, he left Congress to command a militia in Westchester. With guidance from Morris, New York approved the Declaration, making the vote unanimous. Morris signed the document in September after he returned to Congress. When British troops occupied New York, they targeted Morrisania, trashing Morris's house and slaughtering his cattle. After the war, Morris served as a judge and restored his estate. He is buried in Mott Haven in his family vault.

Among the fifty-six signers, eight were immigrants born in England, Ireland, Scotland or Wales. These include Francis Lewis of New York, born in Wales; Button Gwinnett of Georgia, born in England; Robert Morris of Pennsylvania, born in England; James Smith of Pennsylvania, born in Ireland; George Taylor of Pennsylvania, born in Ireland; Matthew Thornton of New Hampshire, born in Ireland; James Wilson of Pennsylvania, born in Scotland; and John Witherspoon of New Jersey, born in Scotland. Since they didn't have American citizenship, are they considered illegal immigrants? Only the Tea Party knows.

Happy Second, Fourth or Ninth of July! Or Second of August?

Brooklyn and the Civil War at 150
April 21, 2011

The Civil War largely spared New York and Brooklyn from military involvement, but the actions of the new president affected the city. Because New York–area politicians had initially been ambivalent and even opposed to war, official attitudes did not fully support the Union cause. Two events brought the Civil War to New York and to Brooklyn, as cited by Bud Livingston in *Brooklyn and the Civil War* (The History Press).

On January 1, 1863, pressured by radical Republicans, Lincoln issued his Emancipation Proclamation. White supremacy agitators charged that this act would activate black migration from the South. The second act was a direct result of Union losses in the early years of the war. Volunteerism slackened with each defeat, so Lincoln ordered institution of a military draft on March 3, 1863, with the first drawing of names on July 10 and the second draft on July 13.

Unfortunately, a provision of the draft stated that a draftee could purchase a substitute for $300, equivalent to a year's salary for a worker. This law transformed the Civil War into a poor man's war. And the poverty-ridden Irish blamed the blacks for this injustice. A man had to own $250 in property to be a citizen, and only citizens could be drafted. Ironically, Tammany had facilitated citizenship for many immigrants in New York. Blacks, who at the time seldom owned property, replaced the draftees in the workplace, thereby being the equivalent of strikebreakers.

The antagonism building between the blacks and the Irish exploded in four days of rioting, with the murder of at least 120 blacks and thousands injured. Most of the mayhem occurred in Manhattan, including burning of the Colored Orphanage on Fifth Avenue and West Forty-fourth Street, but Brooklyn shared the pains of the outrage. Many African Americans fled to Brooklyn for safety, but riots erupted on DeKalb Avenue, and rioters burned grain elevators in Atlantic Basin, causing over $1 million in damage.

Eventually, African Americans fought in the Civil War, with over 180,000 enlisted "colored troops" (USCT), as did the "Fighting Irish" Brigade, the Sixty-ninth Infantry. The first Brooklyn regiment became the famous Eighty-fourth New York Volunteers, known as the Red Legged Devils for their Zouave uniforms. Two Brooklyn camps—Camp Wyman at Fort Hamilton and Camp Maine in East New York—trained forty thousand volunteers.

Statues of Henry Ward Beecher and Abraham Lincoln outside Plymouth Church. *Photo by John Manbeck.*

Brooklyn's prime contribution to the war effort became its Sanitary Fair in 1864, a fundraising campaign that collected $450,000 for Union causes. Brooklyn-born Walt Whitman volunteered as a war nurse.

At this 150th anniversary, many original players and sites can be found around town. For openers, there's the abolitionist preacher Reverend Henry Ward Beecher standing outside his Congregational Plymouth Church of the Pilgrims on Orange Street. He can also be found facing Borough Hall in Columbus Park. Well, his statue anyway.

Inside the church, embedded on the arm of a fourth-row pew, is a brass plate indicating where Abraham Lincoln sat during a sermon the day before making his anti-slavery speech at Cooper Union that won him the presidency.

Today, Brooklyn remembers the issue of slavery with the 2008 establishment of the Brooklyn Abolition Trail to honor the escape route on the slaves' "underground railway" and the preservation of the Duffield Street houses at 227 Abolitionist Place.

Two of Brooklyn's cemeteries also pay tribute to the Civil War. Cypress Hills, on the Brooklyn-Queens border, became the first national cemetery created by Lincoln in 1862. It houses the Union Burial Ground as well as

Confederate graves. Over at Green-Wood Cemetery are monuments to sixteen Union generals, two Confederate generals and thousands of soldiers. Abolitionist publisher Horace Greeley and activists James and Abby Gibbons are also buried in Green-Wood.

Civil War monuments can also be found in Greenpoint and Prospect Heights. The Monitor Monument in Monsignor McGolrick Park celebrates the ironclad warship USS *Monitor*, which was constructed at Greenpoint's shipyards in 1862 before being floated down to the Brooklyn Navy Yard to be outfitted for its battle with the Confederate gunboat *Merrimac*.

Soldiers and Sailors Arch stands at what was originally designed in 1865 and constructed in 1870 as Prospect Park Plaza. In 1892, the triumphal arch rose over the plaza, with the four-horse chariot group by Frederick MacMonnies added on top. The sculptures in tribute to Civil War soldiers and sailors appeared in 1901. As a result of these designs reflecting the Civil War, the plaza was renamed Grand Army Plaza in 1926 as an honor to the Union army, "the Grand Army of the Republic."

Still more Civil War memories remain with us, some causing discomfiture. Politicized by Tammany Democrats, New York gloried in racist "copperhead" attitudes. Their sympathies largely remained with the South because of commercial ties with textiles and finance. The Democrat-backed *Brooklyn Eagle* published pejorative editorials about blacks, particularly against Frederick Douglass. While many New Yorkers and Brooklynites volunteered for the first Union call to arms in August 1862, protesters against the war tried to burn down a South Brooklyn (Red Hook) tobacco warehouse owned by the Lorillard family "in which negroes were employed."

At the end of the war, Beecher reentered the picture when Lincoln chose him to represent the president at an 1865 ceremony to restore the flag at Fort Sumter in South Carolina. And that's where this war began, on April 12, 1862, with the attack on the fort and the Union surrender to Confederate soldiers. While tensions remain taut in Washington these days, preservation of the Republic still remains paramount.

A Night to Remember: Barbara Rodman Wilson
March 20, 2011

A few weeks ago, I gave a talk on the neighborhoods of Brooklyn to the University Club of Long Island. Before the event, I was seated at a table with Barbara Rodman Wilson, who was answering questions about a long-ago event. I became intrigued with her story, particularly when I discovered that her birthday was December 13, 1914.

She piqued my interest when she said that she had spent a night in a leaky lifeboat in 1939. I looked at this woman of ninety-six who possessed such a sharp mind and I remembered the Hitchcock film *Lifeboat*—a film that I learned she refused to see—and of the opening scene of a newer film, *Titanic*, in which an old woman recounts her story of the sinking of an ocean liner.

Wilson's saga unfolded in the archival pages of the *Brooklyn Eagle* and in other contemporary national and local papers. It was the story of a feisty young woman who denied the label "heroine" but who was named Woman of Distinction in 2009. Her story demonstrates the strength of women in history.

Barbara Rodman, her maiden name, survived the sinking of the *Athenia* on September 3, 1939. The *Athenia* was the first passenger ship sunk by torpedoes from a German U-boat. At the time, Rodman was twenty-three and trying to escape the opening stages of World War II. In August, she and a friend had planned a six-week tour of England, France and Germany, but the friend backed out. Rodman set out alone. Once she arrived in England, she realized the precarious and frightening aspects of the world situation. She booked the first voyage available on "any ship crossing the Atlantic," which was the SS *Athenia*, destined for Montreal, Canada.

After the Czechoslovakia fiasco in September 1938, Britain and France issued an ultimatum to Germany, which had threatened to invade Poland. On September 1, 1939, German armies marched into Poland. On the same day, the *Athenia*, a British liner under the command of Captain James Cook, sailed from Glasgow and stopped at Liverpool, where Rodman, a third-class passenger, boarded. About 1,400 other passengers and crew members were accompanying her on this voyage of escape. On September 3, Britain and France declared war on Germany. That night, a stewardess persuaded the seasick Rodman to try the chicken dinner in the dining room. At 7:30 p.m., she checked her watch just as a torpedo tore through the engine room, also demolishing her cabin. It was the first shot fired in World War II. Darkness enveloped her as furniture, dishes and bodies caromed around the dining room. Struggling in spite of bruised legs, she made it to the main deck, where someone threw her a life jacket and directed her to a rope ladder. Throngs of passengers, including many women and children, crowded near

Brooklyn Eagle article on Barbara Rodman Wilson. *Brooklyn Eagle.*

the railing. A sailor guided her, tossing her purse in the water. "Never mind that, lady. Save yourself."

Climbing down the ladder, she found the bottom tangled, and the impatient man behind her kept stepping on her fingers. As another rope snaked by her from above, the young woman who had excelled in athletics at Wellesley lunged for the rope and shimmied down to the lifeboat. There she joined thirty-four other survivors in a leaky boat under the command of the library steward. His mission was to steer the lifeboat through thirty-five- to forty-five-foot waves without capsizing. They were sixty miles south of the Rockall Banks off Ireland.

In the boat, the stopper for the bunghole was missing, as was the bailing bucket. To substitute, passengers plugged the hole with their clothes. "Modesty was not an issue," said Wilson. "I never thought I would live" in those rough seas and rainy weather. All night she was cold, wet and sick—"all alone in the rough water in a leaking boat."

At 5:30 the next morning, lights of rescue ships appeared. The *Athenia* was listing but still afloat. It sank at 10:40 a.m. Two British destroyers, a Swedish yacht, a Norwegian tanker and an American tanker responded to the distress calls. A German liner, *Bremen*, was in the vicinity but did not acknowledge.

After the war, the explanation emerged of the tragedy in which ninety-eight passengers and nineteen crew members had died. With the outbreak of hostilities, German U-boats had been patrolling North Atlantic shipping lanes. Because of the potential danger, the *Athenia* was running without lights and on a zigzag course. This action raised suspicions of the German captain, Lemp, as he tracked the *Athenia*. Deciding that it was a warship, he fired three torpedoes, one of which struck the port side. But he then realized his mistake. According the maritime laws, he should have boarded the *Athenia*, but he left the scene. Nazi officials denied responsibility and changed the records because they didn't want America in the war. Instead, they accused the British of sinking the *Athenia* to drag the neutral United States into the war, despite the fact that twenty-eight Americans had died in the incident. Former president Herbert Hoover doubted that the "clumsy Germans" would have sunk the ship.

Rodman was listed among the dead in the first reports of only sixty-nine survivors. *Eagle* headlines read "Anguished Kin Keep Vigil in Hope and Fear" and "Parents and Friends of L.I. Girl On *Athenia* Keep Anxious Vigil." But Rodman had been rescued by the British destroyer HMS *Escort*. She initially thought the destroyer a German ship, and when she saw a blond sailor, she cursed him as a "dirty ol' German." Then he invited her

Barbara Rodman Wilson, 2010. *Photo by John Manbeck.*

for a spot of tea. For a while, she "hated the Germans' guts," until she married one.

When she landed at Brasco, Scotland, near Glasgow, Rodman received ten shillings to buy a comb and toothbrush. A frightfully colored donated coat with a belt in the back kept her warm. She quickly became a star. The BBC asked her to recount her adventures (available at www.bbc.co.uk/archive), and NBC in New York drove her parents to its studios to talk with their daughter over the wireless. (TV was years away.)

An American ship was sent to bring the survivors home, and newspapers celebrated their homecoming. Rodman's physical injuries healed in months, but the nightmares lasted much longer. Today, she can recite the details of the ordeal but can never relive it.

Her life resumed. When her Springfield, Massachusetts fiancé was killed in the D-Day invasion, she joined the Red Cross and returned to Europe, sailing this time on the *Queen Mary.* She served in England, France and Germany, rehabilitating wounded servicemen.

After the war, she worked for Liebmann Breweries, brewers of Rheingold Beer, as an executive secretary in the Bushwick/Williamsburg section of Brooklyn. There she met Robert Wilson in the 1940s when she was twenty-eight, married him and moved to Garden City. Together they toured Europe, including Germany, but she always felt "apprehensive" about sea travel.

She moved on to work for the Rockefeller Foundation and used her athletic prowess to play tennis at the Garden City Casino. She earned tennis trophies there in the 1950s, but she no longer goes "to dances since I broke my hip last year."

Now a widow, Wilson never had children but has a niece and nephew who helped her celebrate her rescue seventy years later with an exhibit at the Garden City Library and an award at the Merrick Library. In 2009, she told her story on NBC's *Today in New York* when she was interviewed by anchor Michael Gargiulo.

Aside from Wilson's collection of articles and memorabilia, a vestige of her experience crept into a 1940 war movie. In *Arise My Love*, starring Ray Milland and Claudette Colbert, the main characters board the *Athenia*, which later sinks.

In a denouement to the Wilson story, the captain of the U-boat that sank the *Athenia*, Oberleutnant Fritz-Julius Lemp, was killed in 1940 in a battle with a British convoy near Iceland. His captured submarine contained German codebooks that helped shorten the war. The Nazi government never admitted that their submarine sank the *Athenia*. Instead, Propaganda Minister Josef Goebbels insisted that a British submarine had done the dirty work to drag America into the war. The truth was finally revealed during the Nuremberg Trials.

Manhattan Beach: At War and Peace
August 21, 2008

On September 1, 1942, U.S. Coast Guard recruits marched into 125 acres of Manhattan Beach Baths, duffels on their shoulders. The L-shaped land was divided into two bases, with 76 acres set aside for a new civilian-based service at the eastern tip.

The U.S. Maritime Service had been established in 1938 under the Coast Guard to train officers and men for the merchant marines. Then President Franklin D. Roosevelt promoted a "lend-lease" program that avoided waging war but shipped supplies to potential allies.

U.S. Coast Guard on parade at Manhattan Beach. *National Archives*.

Now with war rattling both coasts, a new merchant marine training station was established at Manhattan Beach on Sheepshead Bay. Its purpose? To train ten thousand civilians as sailors to man the new Liberty ships needed to supply American troops. The first graduates shipped out on December 5, 1942, under the War Shipping Administration.

Barracks, a parade ground, a gymnasium, a chapel, an officers' club and a full-sized ship's deck replaced sports, fun and sunbathing. Even the powerhouse qualified as a practice ship's engine room. The pools used for recreation qualified as a training post to teach volunteers from the landlocked Midwest how to swim. Streets were named after naval heroes. Along the eastern shore where Oriental Beach once stood, lifeboat davits hung on a new wall for "Abandon ship" preparation.

Apprentice seamen went through a preliminary six-week training course and were then specialized as members of the deck, engine, kitchen, purser, hospital corps or radio staffs. A real brig, which included a solitary confinement cell, stood near the old Rainbow Bandshell for misbehaving trainees. Seamen also received training in basic gunnery, although guns on merchant ships were handled by U.S. Navy Armed Guard personnel. The merchant marine base processed over 115,000 civilian seamen, half of the nation's volunteer sailors.

Adjoining the merchant marine base on the ocean side stood the U.S. Coast Guard training station, where boxer Jack Dempsey put recruits through several rounds. At the Coast Guard base were a parade ground, barracks and a beach for lifeboat exercises. The Coast Guard trained over one-third of its personnel at the Brooklyn base. Next to the base was the Brooklyn Veterans' Hospital, until a larger one was constructed in Dyker Beach.

Both bases closed at the end of World War II, but City and State Parks Commissioner Robert Moses requested the land for a state park. He received only the beach as a city park. The U.S. Air Force, the New York National Guard, the Civilian Air Patrol and, eventually, veterans' housing utilized the merchant marine barracks until Kingsborough Community College was founded in 1964. Encouraged by Manhattan Beach activist Herman Field and Brooklyn Borough President Abe Stark, the federal government and the city donated the sixty-four-acre campus to the City University of New York for a token fee of one dollar.

Navy Yard Museum Under Full Sail
June 27, 2012

On the foundation of the marine commandant's residence (built in 1855 but uninhabited for seventy-five years), a fabulous Brooklyn Navy Yard Museum opened last year. Other miracles are scheduled for the not-too-distant future.

Since three-quarters of the earth's surface is water, man learned to sail before he perfected the wheel, steam power or jets. And because New York City is composed of three islands, nautical transportation became crucial. In 1802, the newly created government understood this necessity, so President John Adams ordered the purchase from John Jackson of a shipyard in Brooklyn located on the edge of Wallabout Bay. "Can do," replied the navy, and so the New-York Naval Yard materialized in Vinegar Hill.

Today, this base is more fondly remembered as the Brooklyn Navy Yard.

The importance of the Navy Yard—its history and its future—is wonderfully documented in the new Brooklyn Navy Yard Museum, which opened its doors on November 11, 2011, in Building 32 at 63 Flushing Avenue and Carlton Street. Free exhibits trace the history of the Navy Yard from the days of the native Lenapes to those of "Rosie the Riveter."

Brooklyn, rich in lumber and manpower, was an apt location for building wooden warships when young America was still being threatened by England.

Exhibit at the Brooklyn Navy Yard Museum. *Photo by John Manbeck.*

After the War of 1812, the naval station continued to grow, commissioning its first vessel in 1819. The yard filled an increasingly significant role in developing the importance of Brooklyn and New York to the new country.

In 1840, new commandant Matthew Perry introduced innovations such as the dry dock and the Naval Lyceum, an institution designed to promote knowledge through lectures coordinated with a library. During the Civil War, the yard participated in the creation of ironclad ships, most notably the *Monitor.* An exhibit of an 1858 cannon represents that era. In 1889, the yard built the USS *Maine*, whose destruction triggered the Spanish-American War in 1898.

While the Navy Yard did not make significant naval history in World War I, which was primarily a land-based conflict, the yard more than made up for it during World War II when it built major warships and converted liners into troop ships in record time. Over seventy-one thousand workers followed a 24/7 schedule. The USS *Arizona*, which was sunk at Pearl Harbor, and the USS *Missouri*, on which the peace treaty with Japan was signed, originated in the Brooklyn Navy Yard. The last ship launch at the yard during World War II was the USS *Kearsage* in 1945.

The museum's exhibits track this history with artifacts from the eighteenth century to the present, including photographs, sketches, video and aural displays and personal stories of workers at the yard and notable individuals who contributed to its evolution. A newsreel from the war years contributed by the Brooklyn Historical Society traces the type of work completed.

In 1965, the last ship, the USS *Duluth*, slid down the ways. Then, with an "Attention All Hands" announcement from the admiral, the Brooklyn Navy Yard was decommissioned in 1966 and transferred to New York City. After constructing over 150 vessels, the days of the Navy Yard in Brooklyn were over. It was doomed to be "trapped in a rust belt."

The problem of how to use the three hundred acres of waterfront real estate faced Mayor John Lindsay. The *Brooklyn Eagle* ran the headline "Navy Yard Begins Biggest Expansion Since WWII." Private shipping interests operated the yard at first but failed to make it a success in 1966. Then the management of the Brooklyn Navy Yard Development Corporation (BNYDC) changed its scope to sectionalize the operation. Steiner Studios introduced a "green area" for new business opportunities with the aim of working with and for the neighboring communities.

The former Brooklyn Naval Hospital (1838–1948), where E.R. Squibb opened an early laboratory, and Officers' Row buildings posed a dilemma. Hidden behind a fence, trees and weeds on Flushing Avenue at the western edge of the yard, the former residences and hospital languished unattended by their custodian, the National Guard. Now as city property, they have been turned over to the nonprofit Navy Yard operations. Unfortunately, many of the buildings are in disrepair due to neglect by the federal government. The current plan is to stabilize the buildings for later reuse.

A supermarket will be added for the underserved Fort Greene neighborhood. Two of the Officers' Row buildings will be preserved for reuse as private businesses. The others will be demolished. Most of the six rusted dry docks and cranes have been converted to private use. The commandant's house, outside the current Navy Yard property, is privately owned.

Much work lies ahead, but the plans for the yard's tenants are progressing under the direction of Andrew Kimball. The future of the museum is rich, too. With over two hundred years of history, only the surface has been touched. Much related history remains off-site in the Library of Congress, the National Archives, the Smithsonian Institution and naval records. Researching this material is a challenge for archivist Daniela Romano and her assistants. In their archival storeroom lie blueprints and drawings of the original two hundred buildings. Among the artifacts is a cast of the bronze gatepost eagles that decorated the entrance in 1898.

The Navy Yard buildings are filled to 90 percent capacity with 240 businesses and classrooms. Steiner Studios, the yard's biggest tenant, is actively producing major films and television shows including *Boardwalk Empire* and the latest *Spiderman* film. The police auto pound on Sands Street is moving and being replaced by a parking lot. The main gate will be restored to its early 1900s look. Former cemetery grounds near the hospital will be transformed into a twenty-acre "media campus."

From the atrium lobby, with its anchor and chain from the USS *Austin*, the museum is a fascinating and educational experience. Two rooms of computers are available for additional research, and the fourth floor has a cafeteria.

The Brooklyn Veterans' Memorial
October 9, 2008

Can anyone direct me to the Brooklyn War Memorial? Probably not, because it's a long-hidden secret right in front of your eyes. No neon lights, no billboards, no directional signs, no borough president saying, "This way, folks!" Some people prefer to ignore it, but that's like ignoring a white elephant standing in your front yard. At the time of its creation, it was one of the largest monuments in the city. The *AIA Guide to New York City* called it "a wall" to complete the plaza. Today, it endures a similar history to that of the Old Stone House before its 1997 rehabilitation, serving as a restroom station and a repository for parks department equipment.

When the Brooklyn Bridge was modernized in 1935, its Washington Street train terminal was removed along with tracks for the Brooklyn Elevated, Kings County Elevated, a trolley car station and blocks of "undesirable" buildings. Suddenly, a great expanse of land revealed itself. Why not create a park, the city fathers reasoned. Furthermore, they would name it after an eminent Brooklyn clergyman, Dr. Samuel Parkes Cadman, to show they meant well.

But because the park was so empty, Parks Commissioner Robert Moses opted for a large auditorium. In spite of the venerable *Brooklyn Eagle* sponsoring a contest for the auditorium's design (and two winners), the building never materialized. Then Moses conceived of a building with a purpose—times five. To honor the heroes of World War II, he would build massive memorials in each of the boroughs. Construction of Brooklyn's

Above: Brooklyn Veterans' Memorial in Cadman Plaza. *Photo by John Manbeck.*

Left: Abe Ginsberg, World War II pilot. *Author's collection.*

memorial began in 1945, just after Japan surrendered, using the winning design of an auditorium with two wings. This was the only memorial structure built in the city.

But the building that emerged in 1951 was a scaled-down version missing the wings. Due to lack of funding, it never flew. Located in Cadman Plaza Park between Cadman Plaza East and West and bordering on Tillary and Johnson Streets, it was not in a highly traversed location. The outside wall honors Brooklynites who died in World War II, while the structure itself is dedicated to the 300,000 Americans who served in that war. Two relief sculptures by Charles Keck flanking the wall outside the doors symbolize victory and family with an inscription that reads in part: "To the heroic men and women who fought for liberty and especially those who sacrificed...." Since a 1977 restoration, the building has sometimes served as a park recreation center as well as a community facility for veterans' groups and arts organizations.

Now people are pressing for a stronger focus for the memorial. Led by former Borough President Howard Golden, a World War II veteran, and current Borough President Marty Markowitz, they want the war memorial to be a veterans' memorial for *all* American wars to which Brooklynites contributed—from the Battle of Brooklyn in the American Revolution through the Battle of the Bulge to the Battle of Baghdad in Iraq. Stories of these wars would be told through programs and exhibits at a state-of-the-art museum. "I am confident we can achieve our dream for the Brooklyn War Memorial building," said Golden.

Support from the private sector will be spearheaded by Robert Catell of National Grid (formerly Keyspan Energy) and Marilyn Gelber of Independence Community Foundation. From the cultural sector, the nearby Brooklyn Historical Society also supports the project. The Brooklyn Parks Department will supervise renovations, including accessibility by the handicapped. This drive may breathe new life into the white elephant in the middle of a park and, hopefully, restore its original purpose. "This extraordinary building needs to be the place that looks back and looks forward," said Gelber. "It should be a place that serves returning vets as well as a place where older vets can gather." She reminded readers that Borough President Golden had sought to reinstate respect and dignity to the War Memorial Building when he supervised restoration of Borough Hall. "It will take a strong partnership between the public and private sectors to achieve his vision," she said. She insisted that they are committed to bringing this future about.

Now that the playground has been refurbished and buildings next to the mall spruced up (the new Hugh Carey Courthouse, the city's new Emergency Headquarters and the historic Post Office Building), it seems time to introduce the war memorial as a true veterans' memorial.

Part XIII

CONEY ISLAND

Down by the Brooklyn Sea
April 23, 2009

Now that advertising is posted for summer lifeguards on city beaches, it's time to think warm. Lifeguards atop tall stands represent safety on our beaches. When beachgoers first ventured onto Brooklyn sands, those lifeguards sat in rowboats to prevent non-swimmers (most of the visitors to Coney Island) from straying into deep waters. As an extra precaution, safety ropes extended beyond the breakers.

Before the big public amusement rides arrived, saltwater bathing attracted the attention of the Victorian public because the mineral content was similar to that of the popular spas—and it was free. It was also cooler than pre–air conditioned summers in the city. In addition, men and women could appear in public in a semi-undressed state. That was enough fun for them.

Society was unsure how to handle this untoward situation. Previously, men had bathed in the ocean naked without female company, while women had used "bathing machines." Now they both wore long underwear.

If you look at nineteenth-century photographs of early Coney Island, the beaches are crowded, but most of the people are standing (not lying on the sand) and are dressed in long dresses, jackets, hats, dress shirts and ties. The same was true for the new popular activity of the nineteenth century: the picnic in the park. These outdoor activities were regarded as formal affairs.

Bathers in Coney Island at the turn of the twentieth century. *Kingsborough Historical Society.*

Those wearing bathing suits had rented them from bathhouses and usually covered them with robes or coats. To take a chance and change behind a bush meant risking having your clothes stolen.

Popular publications offered lengthy advice for visiting the beach, both practical and moral. Doctors advised covering up as much as possible because of the dangers of the sun, words of wisdom that we're only heeding a century later. (The appearance of Jantzen and Catalina bathing suits in 1930s movies changed our minds about exposing skin.) They also recommended changing from wet suits as soon as possible to avoid catching a cold, although a wet, itchy, smelly suit might be a better reason. Most bathing suits covered the body from neck to ankle, with shoes to protect (and cover) the feet. In an account in a contemporary newspaper, a young lady rejected a suitor because she saw his ugly toes.

Most visitors were fearful of the water and did not know how to swim. They clung to safety ropes and bobbed up and down in the waves. Swimmers had more leeway with lighter (and more revealing) suits that featured tops only to the elbows and knee-length bottoms so they could be more active. Those who did not dress appropriately were subject to arrest by the beach patrol. The same rules applied to both men and women.

Bathhouses usually had a nefarious reputation because the shacks generally had cracks and knotholes, preventing privacy, and because the suits could not be guaranteed to have been suitably cleaned between uses. As time passed, larger bathhouses appeared in addition to those attached to the larger hotels. In advertisements, these establishments guaranteed bathing suits to be cleaned between uses by the latest washing machines. The Manhattan Beach Hotel even had scented changing rooms with live music supplied by caged canaries.

Coney Island had no extended boardwalk then—only limited walks in front of individual hotels, which were constructed down to the waterline. Eventually, the mores changed, and practical advice prevailed. After several hotels collapsed in the sand due to erosion, they were moved back to safety. Then, in 1923, the current boardwalk was built as a divider and bulwark against the ocean. The newer bathhouses—Stauch's, Ward's, Washington, etc.—were self-contained, with dining and dancing facilities included in the membership, as well as private pools and game areas. However, only behind those fences could men remove the tops of their bathing suits.

Until the mid-1930s, persons who strayed beyond the gates of the private baths had to adhere to the blue laws of the city. Men had to wear not only tops but also robes to walk on the boardwalk. Otherwise, they had to cross under the boardwalk if they wished to swim in the ocean.

Nowadays, there are rumors that Coney Island is dead. Not true. Amusement rides, such as Astroland, are gone, but the beach is still alive and well. Amusements come and go. Sea Lion Park, Dreamland, Luna Park, Steeplechase, Brighton Beach Park, Bergen Beach Park and Golden City Park were all summer amusement parks in Brooklyn. No longer.

Soon, the Mermaid Parade will surface, and those lifeguards will return to their stands, noses white, sunglasses dark. As long as there's water in the sea, bathers will make their annual treks to the ocean.

So come on down!

Life-Saving Service
April 30, 2009

As I reported in last week's column, nineteenth-century bathing differed greatly from what goes on at our beaches today. To the Victorians, beach going was a whole new ballgame, so to speak. So was lifesaving, for the average beachgoer knew nothing about swimming. With good reason, they never strayed far from the safety ropes.

But there were lifesavers whose jobs reeked of danger. Instead of balmy beaches, they worked in winter and during violent storms. They were federal employees

Life-saving station at Manhattan Beach. *Kingsborough Historical Society/Long Island Historical Society.*

of the U.S. Life-Saving Service. Their responsibility was to rescue victims of shipwrecks, as most wooden ships splintered when they dashed upon rocks.

The lifesaver, as opposed to the lighthouse keeper, searched reefs along the shore for stranded survivors. He also rowed out to wrecks in his lifeboat to save victims and property, if necessary.

Off Brooklyn's southern shore, the treacherous Rockaway reefs between Coney Island and the Rockaways proved a most dangerous graveyard for schooners. In the 1850s, Secretary of War Jefferson Davis (yes, the same one) mandated that a life-saving station be erected on the sandy coast of Pelican Island, now Manhattan Beach. In actuality, the station was a two-story house built for the lifesaver and his family. Generally, life on the beach was tranquil in clear weather, but storm clouds prompted the family to batten down the hatches and for the lifesaver to put on his slicker, grab his lantern and brave the elements. While life on shore was safer than at sea, reports circulated of the "surfman's" home being swept out to sea when the father returned from his rounds. On March 16, 1889, the life-saving station at Far Rockaway, across Jamaica Bay, was destroyed in a violent storm.

While the U.S. Life-Saving Service had its own emblem since its origin in 1848, it was separate from lighthouse keepers and from the U.S. Coast Guard. Before that date, the rescue service had been private and local. Eventually, Congress merged the service into the Revenue Cutter Service and then into the U.S. Coast Guard in 1915. It originated in the Newell Act, which established initially unmanned stations along the New Jersey coast, New York harbor and the Massachusetts coastline to provide "surf boats, rockets, carronades and other necessary apparatus" to save lives from shipwrecks.

After the fury of a hurricane that hit the Carolinas in 1854, Congress appropriated additional funds for better training, more supervision and manned stations. But they still lacked adequately trained personnel because it was largely a volunteer service. In 1874, the service was placed under the Department of Treasury, with new stations added in Maine, Cape Cod, the Outer Banks, the Great Lakes, Florida and Texas.

By 1915, the Life-Saving Service consisted of over 270 stations along the Atlantic coast. At that point, President Woodrow Wilson signed a bill merging the service into the U.S. Coast Guard. During its existence, the service saved 178,741 persons from drowning.

Related to the lifesaver is the lighthouse keeper. Because of Brooklyn's sixty-four miles of coastline, lighthouses performed a safety function as well. Initially independent, the U.S. Coast Guard also supervised lighthouse operations after 1939. In Brooklyn, the most famous lighthouse is located in Sea Gate and was built in 1890. Functioning long after other lighthouses were automated, it too was finally mechanized in 1989. Frank Schubert, the keeper of the Coney Island Light, was the last civilian lighthouse keeper in the United States. He died in 2003.

Other lights are visible from Brooklyn or nearby viewing sites. Over in Staten Island, two lighthouses exist: the Staten Island Light (1912) and the light at Fort Wadsworth (1903). The most important light we don't consider a navigational tool, but that's what the Statue of Liberty (1885) originally was.

A variation of a lighthouse, the Ambrose Lightship, can be spotted on the other side of the East River. A lightship was authorized for the Ambrose Channel in 1823 and was stationed there until 1967, when the Ambrose Tower replaced it. The tower was dismantled in 2008 after it was damaged by a freighter. Illuminated buoys now safeguard the channel.

The Ambrose Lightship that rests in South Street Seaport served in the channel from 1908 until 1933. Retired in 1964, South Street Seaport acquired it in 1968. In 1989, the government declared it a National Historic Landmark. The last lightship used in the Ambrose Channel is berthed in Boston Harbor.

The newest light used for official navigational purposes appeared in the 1990s atop a new marine center on the beachside campus of Kingsborough Community College in Manhattan Beach.

And the light still shines.

Carl Looff and Coney's Carousels
April 2, 2009

As Coney Island slowly sinks in the south along with the sunset, images of past remain as phantasmagoria, as the lights of Luna Park, the whiteness of Dreamland and the buffoonery of Steeplechase combine with screams from Hell Gate and roller coasters, the multitude of bathhouses and restaurants, the Parachute Jump and AstroTower. Sure, the Cyclone and Wonder Wheel still operate (courtesy of the landmark law), but at best they are shadows of another world.

While most people associate Coney Island with thrill rides, modest artistry also began there. Numerous elegant and dignified carousels graced almost every block, and these creations set the tone for later amusements. Talented artisans created magnificent horses and rides that lured the child in us all. The earliest in Coney Island came from the imagination of Charles Looff in 1876.

Certainly the most successful, Looff blazed a trail for those who studied with him and followed him: Illions, Carmel, Mangels, Stein and Goldstein.

Sign for a Looff carousel. *Photo by John Manbeck.*

Most of these woodcarvers apprenticed in Europe. Born in Denmark in 1852, Looff immigrated to New York in 1870, changed his name from Carl to Charles and found work as a carver in a Greenpoint furniture factory. In his spare time, he carved wooden horses on assembled platforms and sold them to Coney Island. In 1876, the carousel appeared at Lucy Vanderveer's Bathing Pavilion, where it offered amusement to customers. Later called Balmer's Pavilion, it was located at Surf Avenue and West Sixth Street, in the heart of Coney. This carousel survived until the 1911 Dreamland fire. So successful was this merry-go-round that Charles Feltman ordered one for his Surf Avenue beer garden in 1877. The Feltman carousel, partially destroyed in a fire, was replaced by a Mangels-Illions carousel.

Branching out, Looff built a Greenpoint factory on Bedford Avenue in 1880 and searched for new markets. The same year, Atlantic City responded by ordering one for Young's Million Dollar Pier, and by 1884, Roger Williams Park in Rhode Island joined the customers. Orders came in from Staten Island; Dartmouth, Massachusetts; Dallas, Texas; upstate New York; Salem, New Hampshire; Port Dalhousie; Ontario, Canada; and San Francisco. Built in 1904, the Zeum Carousel survived the 1906 San Francisco earthquake while traveling to Seattle, Washington, and then to Roswell, New Mexico, for restoration before finally returning to its home at Yerba Buena Park in 1998.

With the increasing business, Looff bought property in Gravesend close to Coney Island and built a factory, hoping to expand a portable carousel line. However, the city decided it wanted to build a park on that site and condemned the property in 1905. This action infuriated Looff, who was forced to move his business to Riverside, Rhode Island. While successful there, he grew restless again and moved to Ocean Park, California, leaving a son to manage the Rhode Island factory. Once in California, Looff shifted his operation to Long Beach and the fabulous amusement center called The Pike that extended onto a pier. The Looff carousel there was destroyed by a fire in 1943 but was replaced with another Looff carousel.

Looff's equine creations reflect a gentle nature, as opposed to the fiery Coney Island steeds of Illions and Carmel. After 1903, Looff began incorporating organs from the Knapp Barrel Organ Works. Expanding, he continued to create and build other amusements, including roller coasters, Ferris wheels and a Whip ride. In 1909, he built a carousel of fifty-four horses as a wedding present for his daughter, Emma Looff Vogel.

Looff died in Long Beach on July 1, 1918, never forgiving Brooklyn politicians. But his reputation and his creations live on around the world, the most recent being ones in Redondo Beach (1925) and Griffith Park (1926). Many surviving carousels have been declared National Historic Landmarks.

But they all started in Brooklyn.

The Circus Comes to Brooklyn
June 11, 2009

Want to run away and join the circus, kid? Brooklyn might be a good place to start, for the circus was a familiar sight in old Brooklyn. And those times may be coming back.

This summer, the famed Ringling Bros. Barnum & Bailey Circus (the 139th edition of the Red Tour) will appear on the boardwalk of fabulous Coney Island from June 17 until September 7, 2009. The show is called "Coney Island Boom-A-Ring." In 2013, the circus will open in Brooklyn's new Barclays Center.

Steeplechase circus in Coney Island, 1936. *Brooklyn Public Library, Brooklyn Collection.*

On the other hand, Coney Island is closer to the carny world than you remember.

In 1835, Barnum opened a "museum" on Broadway and Prince Street in which he introduced a blind, paralyzed black woman, Joice Heth, as George Washington's 160-year-old nurse. (At her death, doctors determined she was in her 80s.) Barnum attracted 400,000 customers a year.

Seven years later, Barnum, in his new museum on Broadway, north of Fulton Street in Manhattan, added more flamboyance and hype. He renamed four-year-old Charles Stratton, a midget, as General Tom Thumb and passed him off for eleven. Twenty years later, he staged Stratton's wedding to Lavina Bump, a lady of his size.

Next he introduced Jenny Lind, a soprano from Sweden whom he had never heard sing. After a year's promotion with dolls, clothes and souvenirs, he finally brought her over here. On September 11, 1850, Lind's Castle Garden concert sold out, with top tickets going for $225, or $6,000 in today's money. He also introduced the first aquarium, the first three-ring circus and a rogues' gallery of wax figures. Chang and Eng were Siamese twins he brought to New York. They, too, became a later hit.

Barnum circus in Bedford-Stuyvesant in 1902. *Brooklyn Public Library, Brooklyn Collection.*

After the Civil War, Barnum moved to Madison Park, where he built Barnum's Great Roman Hippodrome on West Twenty-third Street and Madison Avenue, present-day site of the Met Life Building. Upon seeing Barnum's success, other entrepreneurs, such as William Coup, started their own circuses. To make his own circus bigger, Barnum teamed up with Coup and began P.T. Barnum's Grand Traveling Museum, Menagerie, Caravan and Hippodrome. In other words, it was a circus that traveled to Brooklyn by barges (no bridge yet) in 1871 and welcomed visitors annually to its tents in Bushwick at Broadway and Halsey Street.

After another merger with James Bailey in 1881, Barnum unpretentiously labeled his Barnum and Bailey circus the "Greatest Show on Earth." He then bought an elephant from the London Zoo that he named Jumbo, and after that, a gorilla named Gargantua. Jumbo made his first appearance in Brooklyn at Fulton Street and Sumner Avenue in 1882 along with twenty-two elephants and Barnum's menagerie. According to the *Brooklyn Eagle*, the opening began with an "imperial triple grand processional in three rings."

When the Brooklyn Bridge opened in 1883, Barnum requested that Jumbo march over it, but he was denied. The next year, however, Jumbo and twenty-one elephants joined a parade in May "in the interest of the dear public." Barnum pronounced the bridge safe to cross. He died in 1891, but other entertainment forces were at work.

In 1892, a Wild West circus opened in Ambrose Park, the site of today's Bush Terminal in Sunset Park. The promoter was Buffalo Bill Cody, whose troupe of cowboys and Indians (led by Sitting Bull) was on its final tour of the states and Europe.

In 1907, Barnum & Bailey merged with Ringling Brothers, returning to Brooklyn in 1917. In 1923, it opened a show in a posh section of Flatlands called Vanderveer Park. Nearby, a golf course sold their land to City University, but while plans were being developed, Ringling Brothers raised its tents near the Flatbush-Nostrand junction in the early 1930s. But by 1935, it had to move on because ground had been broken for a new Brooklyn College—not exactly a circus act.

So cheer when you hear that circus fanfare—the circus is back in Brooklyn town!

Ghosts of Brooklyn
June 25, 2009

As we look around Brooklyn today, we slowly notice that once-familiar surroundings disappear amid signs of continuing stability. A store, a name, familiar faces—we realize that they no longer rest in our subconscious awareness. Only vacant storefronts and new, unfamiliar names remain. We are shocked that they never even wished us farewell.

It seems unfathomable to conceive the northern edge of Brooklyn, where Brooklyn Bridge Park rises, as home to seventy steamship lines, yet that is the figure given in the *Official Brooklyn Guide* published in 1939.

Fulton Street is rife with memories, sometimes with reminders embedded in granite, such as the "OC" on the roof of the former Oppenheim Collins department store building or the plaque outside Macy's reminding passersby that it was once the Abraham & Straus Department Store. Then there's the ghostly lettering painted on the side of the former Hotel Montague on Montague Street or the "To Let" sign on Middagh Street off Henry.

Stories about Brooklyn's famed "Downtown" Fulton Street, lined with Loeser's, Namm's, A&S, Martin's and Oppenheim Collins, have been written by me and others. The same is true of the theaters—both theatrical and cinema—that lined Flatbush Avenue. Remember Loew's Metropolitan, Brooklyn Paramount, Brooklyn Fox, RKO Albee, Brooklyn Strand, Orpheum or the Majestic? Only the Majestic survives, but now it's The Harvey. The vicinity also claimed to be the culinary center long before Smith Street reigned, with the Brass Rail next to the Strand Cafeteria, a fast-food restaurant. The elite Gage & Tollner's, with its gas-lit interior, commanded Fulton Street for a century, while the Horn & Hardart Automat lodged across the street, where Burger King now stands.

Other eateries prevailed, and we have an eclectic variety of international restaurants stacked along Montague Street. Who remembers Foffe's, a second-story walkup? (The name remains etched on the glass transom.) How about Joe's, on what used to be called Fulton Street (now Cadman Plaza) between Pierrepont and Montague? Farther down on Henry Street near Clark was Patricia Murphy's Candlelight Restaurant, famous for its popovers. The address was 114 Henry Street, a site vacated more recently by a Thai restaurant. Patricia Murphy's, a chain with additional locations in midtown Manhattan, Long Island, Westchester and Florida, catered to women just as Schrafft's did over on Jay Street.

While the new Sheraton rises on Duffield Street, the New York Marriott at Brooklyn Bridge now seems to be a grand old lady. But remains of even older hotels still exist, although today they serve as condos or offices. In 1939, visitors could reserve rooms at the Hotel St. George, the Towers, the Bossert, Hotel Margaret, the Touraine, the Standish Arms or the Sir Henry Apartment Hotel. Across from the Brooklyn Academy of Music, the Granada served before- and after-theater drinks, and Coney Island had its specter of the Half Moon Hotel on the Boardwalk.

But how about other ghosts? On the apex of the triangle across from the recently merged Washington Mutual/JPMorgan Chase/Dime Savings Bank stood Weber & Heilbroner, an exclusive men's clothing store. Around the corner on Flatbush Avenue was Bond's, which offered not-so-affluent men's wear. And over on Livingston Street, in the educational art store next to Dallas BBQ, one could find the "plain pipe racks" of Robert Hall Clothes. More recently, a Korvette's was spotted on Fulton Street. What ever happened to the used book dealers

Brooklyn's Famous Eating Place

JOE'S RESTAURANT • 326-334 Fulton Street, Brooklyn, New York

Postcard of Joe's Restaurant on Court Street. *Author's collection.*

on Willoughby Street? Did Nobody Beats the Wiz join Crazy Eddie in hucksters' heaven? Easy come, easy go.

Admittedly, some of these former behemoths were not Brooklyn-born, but they affected Brooklynites just as the loss of neighborhood drugstores did. (Check out the corner storefront entrance on Middagh and Hicks Streets for the word "drugs" in the tile.) Then there were the neighborhood grocery stores and candy stores and smaller supermarkets such as Bohack's (on Henry Street and Love Lane), A&P and Roulston's, having been replaced by all-purpose Duane Reade, CVS, Rite-Aid and other "convenience" stores.

Borden's and Renken's delivered milk to homes, as did Dugan's Bakery—just like the *New York Times* delivers its newspaper now. But that too might be a fleeting memory. The UP (United Press) was once a wire service, just as AP (Associated Press) is now. Western Union has become a shadow of its former self but still exists at UPS stores (for money orders). Railway Express, with offices at the Atlantic Avenue's Long Island Terminal (pardon me, Barclays Center) has disappeared, though.

While it appears that Brooklyn boasts a surfeit of financial establishments, how many of these 1939 banks still exist? Now names like Brooklyn Savings Bank, Dime Savings Bank, People's Savings Bank, Corn Exchange

Bank, South Brooklyn Savings Institution, Kings Highway Savings Bank, Bushwick Savings Bank, Flatbush Savings Bank, Flatlands Savings and Loan Co., Williamsburgh Savings Bank, Roosevelt Savings Bank or Greenpoint Savings Bank are only memories.

In 1939, Brooklyn boasted seven radio stations and at least four newspapers: *Brooklyn Daily Eagle, Coney Island Times, Brooklyn Citizen* and the *Chat*.

Before World War II, Brooklyn supported a vibrant business community. Today, most of these 1939 names no longer identify with our borough: Royal Baking Powder, Kirkman's Soap, Brillo, A&P Coffee, Higgin's Inks, Mongol Pencils, Ex-Lax, Mason's Mints, Gem Razors, Schraders' Valves, Bond Bread, Bond Clothes, Lily Cups, Trommer's Beer, Rheingold Beer, Schaffer's Beer, Detecto Scales, Gretsch Musical Instruments, Pfizer Chemicals, Barracini Chocolates, Mangel Carousels, Sperry Gyroscopes, Halvah, Bonomo Taffy, Ebinger Bakery, Dugan's Bread, Borden's Milk, Renkin's Milk, Brooklyn Union Gas, Brooklyn Borough Gas, New York Dock Company, Amstar Sugar (Domino), Fox's U-Bet, Manhattan Special Coffee, AriZona Tea, SoHo Natural Soda, Topps Gum, Chiclets Gum, Sweet'N Low, Twizzlers, Howard Clothes, Abe Stark Suits.

A Canadian company has overtaken our own Brooklyn Union Gas Company, but before National Grid, a Brooklyn Borough Gas existed down in Coney Island, just as other small firms made up Consolidated Edison (which is why "union" and "consolidated" are in their titles). When heating a home by coal was cool, Blue Coal sponsored a radio show called *The Shadow*, and Koppers Koke (cute name) polluted Coney Island Creek.

On the more stable side, the original Häagen-Dazs has managed to survive on Montague Street since 1976.

Now most these names have been relegated to the dustbins of our memories. But the next generation will have their memories to dredge up to regale their bored grandchildren with stories about their old days and the funny names: cell phones, American Idol, tattoos, McDonald's, gasoline and newspapers.

AFTERWORD

"Ya oughta play fuh da Bushwicks, ya bum ya!" That insult would be heaped from the stands at Ebbets Field on a Dodger who had misplayed a ball or ignominiously left base runners stranded. The Bushwicks were a semi-pro team from one of Brooklyn's multitudinous neighborhoods.

Brooklyn then, as John Manbeck notes, was a baseball town, and the game was the one link connecting its disparate sections in what was no longer an independent city. "Only the dead know Brooklyn," Thomas Wolfe had written, explaining that no living mortal could master the borough's vast, diverse and confusing geography. Brooklyn—bits of it—filled my own blood even though I was born in Finland. My mother had been born in Flatbush, and her parents ran a weekly paper for Swedish-speaking immigrants from Finland out of the "Finntown" blocks in what is now Sunset Park but was then part of a generic "South Brooklyn" covering the expanse between Atlantic Avenue and Bay Ridge.

After returning to marry an engineer in Finland, Mother brought me at age seven to visit her mother and siblings, who were living on Parade Place overlooking the Parade Ground, then alive with baseball games on its many diamonds. That was my first glimpse of the game. Three years later, we came here to live, and I quickly became a Dodger fan. The team sponsored a "Knothole Gang" for youngsters, who were granted admission to the bleacher seats for ten cents. I got to know most of the players even in their civilian clothes while hanging around for autographs outside the hotels in Brooklyn Heights, where they were billeted during the

Henrik Krogius. *Photo by Elaine Taylor Krogius.*

season. Now we have only the minor-league Cyclones. The real focus has shifted to basketball. We are waiting to see if the Nets and Barclays Center will truly do for Brooklyn what the Dodgers and Ebbets Field once did. On a cultural level, the Brooklyn Academy of Music (BAM) and the burgeoning arts center around it have conferred a new elite aura on Brooklyn, abetted by clusters of artists taking over rundown former industrial areas. Gourmet eateries have also sprung up, and beer is again being brewed here. Still, these factors don't add up to the kind of popular unifying presence that was represented by the Dodgers.

When Henry Stiles produced his *History of the City of Brooklyn* (1867–70), that city was much newer and rather more compact than the current borough, but it had a distinct identity. Now only a borough, albeit the most populous one in the City of New York, Brooklyn has endured living in the shadow of Manhattan. A new "history" of this place has been struggling to emerge. The late Elliot Willensky tried to make the case for a "golden age" of the borough in his extravagantly titled 1986 book *When Brooklyn Was the World, 1920–1957* (Crown), though he confessed that the borough "lost its confidence" well before 1957, the year the Dodgers left. Yet a certain Brooklyn mystique has never quite been extinguished. In 1991, the *New York Times* art critic Grace Glueck and Paul Gardner turned out a handsome coffee-table book, *Brooklyn: People and Places, Past and Present* (Harry Abrams), that saw the borough as symbolizing "those very American qualities of ambition, brashness, wiseguy humor, street smarts, and underneath the toughness, a soft touch." Although light on Brooklyn's grittier aspects, the book provided a wide historical miscellany. Brian Merlis, the Brooklyn Historical Society and others have published photographic records of various individual Brooklyn neighborhoods accompanied by historical text.

So, even as a resurgent Brooklyn gains increasing notice and respect in the wider world, it is perhaps wrong to ask that its story be told in any single, conventional, summarizing book. Historians have by and large come to recognize that history has many more strands, many more separate stories, than earlier practitioners gave serious credence to. John Manbeck, taking it facet by facet, has been building a grand mosaic of Brooklyn and its history. In his volume, he has added more tiles to the mosaic pattern of his earlier volume, *Brooklyn: Historically Speaking*. For Brooklyn, so rich in diversity, that seems the most promising and rewarding way to go.

—*Henrik Krogius*

INDEX

ABOUT THE AUTHOR

John B. Manbeck, professor emeritus from Kingsborough Community College and former Brooklyn Borough Historian, is author/editor of seven books on Brooklyn, including *Brooklyn: Historically Speaking* (The History Press). In addition, he contributed to *The Encyclopedia of New York City, 2 nd Edition* and *The Encyclopedia of New York State*. He has held several city- and state-appointed positions and serves on advisory and foundation boards. In 1965, he taught for two years at Helsinki University (Finland) on a Fulbright scholarship. His weekly column, "Historically Speaking," the basis of this book, ran for eight years in the *Brooklyn Daily Eagle*. His first e-book is a novella, *Death on the Rise*, published on Kindle. His website, www. johnbmanbeck.net, is registered with the Authors' Guild.